The Collected Poems
of
Richard Francis Towndrow

Valericain Press

Valericain
Press

Copyright © 2023 by **Chris Towndrow**

All rights reserved. No part of this publication may be reproduced, distributed or transmitted in any form or by any means, without prior written permission.

No generative artificial intelligence (AI) was used in the writing of this work. The author expressly prohibits any entity from using this publication for purposes of training AI technologies to generate text, including without limitation technologies that are capable of generating works in the same style or genre as this publication. The author reserves all rights to license uses of this work for generative AI training and development of machine learning language models.

The Collected Poems of Richard Francis Towndrow

Hardcover ISBN: 978-1-7384470-3-9
Paperback ISBN: 978-1-7384470-2-2
Amazon Hardcover ISBN: 978-1-7392306-6-1
Amazon Paperback ISBN: 978-1-7392306-4-7
eBook ISBN: 978-1-7392306-5-4

First edition August 2023
Second edition November 2023

Valericain Press
Richmond, London, UK
www.valericainpress.co.uk

Table Of Contents

Foreword 11
About The Author 15
SECTION 1 : 'A Life, Love and other poems' 19
DEDICATION 21
PREFATORY NOTE TO "LOVE." 22
A LIFE 23
PART I - DEATH-IN-LIFE 25
PART II. - LIFE-IN-DEATH 29
PART III. - THE AWAKENING 35
PART IV. - HOPE 41
LOVE 49
TO LOVE. (1 COR. XIII. 13.) 51
TO LOVE'S SOURCE. (I JOHN IV. 7.) 109
SHORTER POEMS 113
A CHARACTER SKETCH 115
MARGARET 116
AMY 118
IDA 119
PASSING 120
SUNLESS 121
IN MEMORIAM. A. M. M. 123
PENELOPE. (A FRAGMENT.) 124
TIME—A RIVER 126
RETROSPECT 128
A MEMORY 130
"For with Thee is the well of life, and in Thy light shall we see light."
- PSALM xxxvi. 9 131

DROWNED	133
TO A.R.W.	134
THE SEARCH	135
TO—	137
A SUMMER DAY	138
THE VISION OF GOD	139
SECTION 2: 'A Garden' and other poems	**145**
A GARDEN	147
THE AURORA BOREALIS (OCTOBER 25, 1870)	150
AN ARTISTS IDEAL	152
A HOLIDAY LYRIC	155
A YEAR'S CHANGES	158
THEO	162
SUN-STEEPED	165
FAILURE?	167
'DOE YE NEXTE THYNGE' (OLD SAXON LEGEND)	168
A WORD OF REMEMBRANCE	169
MAY-DAY	170
IN KEMPSEY CHURCH	172
SONG	174
A POOL IN A MEADOW	176
A WORD UNSAID	178
DARKNESS AND LIGHT	179
SONNETS OF THE SEASONS	182
TO THE AUTHOR OF "EMPIRE"	190
ON GUSTAV DORE'S PICTURE, "PAOLO AND FRANCESCA DI RIMINI"	191
ON MALVERN HILLS	192
A SHELTER	193

MUTABILITY	194
SOLITUDE	195
OUT OF THE PAST	196
THE HEART AND THE TREASURE	197
HUMAN INABILITY (ON SOME ATTEMPTED STATEMENTS OF TRUTH)	198
VEILED	199
UNVEILED	200
A MAN	201
ANOTHER MAN	202
A WOMAN	203
AN IDEAL	204
DEVELOPMENT	205
UNSPEAKABLE	206
ON RUTHLESS EXPLORATION	207
"MISSED HIS VOCATION" (A disputed Verdict)	208
LOSSES	209
SATISFIED	210
SLEEP	211
SECTION 3: Sonnets Of Love, Life, and Death	**217**
A REFUTATION	218
LOVE'S CONQUEST	219
A JOURNEY	220
LOVE'S CRY	222
SECTION 4: Rare & Unpublished Poems	**229**
YOU AND I	231
SPRING: A DREAM FULFILLED	232
A GLASTONBURY THORN (Flowering in the garden of the Swan Inn, Newland, Worcestershire, on Christmas Day 1903)	234

AN EVENING HYMN	235
A GOLDEN WEDDING	237
THROUGH THE YEARS	238
THE TRIO	239
ON MALVERN HILLS (Alternative version)	240
EVERLASTING FLOWERS	242
HEALING	243
THE CRY OF THE HILLS	245
AFTER MANY YEARS	246
TO OUR TULIP TREE (Thornbank School)	247
AFTER MANY DAYS	248
AFTER MANY DAYS (Alternative version)	249
MAY	250
SONNET ("Not far from every one of us")	251
THE COMING OF SPRING	252
VITA NUOVA (The First Buttercup)	253
A HOME RULER (THE CRISIS)	254
AT THE ROLL OF HONOUR	255
LOVE'S CRY (Unpublished version)	256
THE COMFORT	257
(Title unknown)	258
THE ABBEY SCHOOL	259
ONE OF LIFE'S PICTURES	261
THE MUSIC OF THE YEARS	262
About The Editor	**273**

Foreword

Richard Francis Towndrow was my great-great grandfather.
He came into my conscious in the late 1990s when I became involved in researching our family tree. This endeavour linked my immediate family with distant relatives around the world, uncovering personalities and stories dating back to the 1600s. As someone who was dabbling in poetry at the time, finding this volume of work written by Richard Francis resonated with me.
It is very much of its time, although I particularly enjoy "On Malvern Hills", being familiar with the area as a result of visits with my family.

As well as poetry, "RFT" also wrote books on botany and a critique of Tennyson's "In Memoriam". I have included a short biography of the man herein.

During a career break in 2004 I undertook to transcribe the poetry from old books and original paper notes that are in the family's possession. These poems were published as two eBooks in 2013.

In the following decade, I devoted much of my spare time to my own fiction writing, and in 2023 I published a novel which quotes a verse of RFT's "Theo" (and refers to the emigration of Towndrows to the USA) and as a result I revisited these old RFT manuscripts.

I decided to combine the eBooks, adding in all the material from two other archive titles, to produce a new volume of all known work. It can be regarded as a "definite edition" of Richard Francis' output.

This collection predominantly contains poems from the published books and as well as some that were never compiled into a book, or even published individually:

Part 1 : "A Life, Love and other poems" (1889)

Part 2: "A Garden and other poems" (1892)

Part 3: "Sonnets of Life, Love, and Death" (1896)

Part 4: Privately circulated or unpublished poems (1896 ff)

The poems in Part 4 are listed chronologically (where the date is known).

During transcription I have retained the original formatting as best as possible, including RTF's indentations and notes. There may, of course, be the odd character or word which is in error or illegible.

I have also included a few photographs of RFT (and wife Corinna), plus facsimiles of original works.

Hopefully the work of Richard Francis Towndrow will find an audience in a new medium and a new century. Notwithstanding, this volume serves to collate and preserve his work in new, more easily accessible and readable formats.

Christopher Harrison Towndrow, 2023

About The Author

The Malvern Gazette published a tribute to Richard Francis Towndrow (29th Oct 1845 – 25th Dec 1937) on January 1st, 1938, which best relates the high esteem with which he was regarded in the community.

The following excerpt is from that account which appears in a treasured archival volume compiled by one of his sons;

"In the death of Mr. Richard Francis Towndrow, which occurred at his residence, Ashville, Malvern Wells, on Christmas Day, Malvern has lost one of its oldest and most esteemed residents. Mr Towndrow, who had been in failing health for some time past, celebrated his 92nd birthday on October 29th last. He was a famous entomologist and botanist, and the senior member and at one time President of Malvern Field Club, in which he took an active part, being regular in his attendance at the Club's excursions while he was able to get about. He was well read in the history of the Malvern Hills and had a wide knowledge of the plant life of the district.

Many years ago Mr Towndrow carried on a grocery and provision establishment in Malvern Link, of which he was a native, and was closely connected with St Matthias' Church, holding office as Vicar's Warden under the Rev. A. Day. On his retirement from business 26 years ago, he went to reside in the Wells, and served as Church warden under the late Archdeacon Walters and the Rev. G.K.M. Green.

A quiet and unassuming man, Mr Towndrow never took a prominent part in public affairs apart from his membership of the Hills Conservancy Board, on which he served for a number of years, retiring only a short time ago.

For a long time he was responsible for the arrangement of the wild flowers which stood in the entrance hall of Malvern Public Library.

For half a century he made a profound study of natural history, and flora in particular. He discovered numerous forms of rare plant life and placed his extensive knowledge and experience at the command of many who compiled and published data concerning the flora of the four counties. When Mr Carlton Rae produced, in 1910, his Addenda to the Botany of Worcestershire, Mr Towndrow's was the first name in the list of local discoverers.

'The Sagina Teuteri Briss, apetala, Malvern, Bickham and Towndrow,' suggests another co-adventure with the late Mr Spencer Harry Bickham of Ledbury, one of his closest friends. In a later but useful work, commenced for the Malvern College Field Club, and issued half a century later as the Malvern Field Handbook, Mr C.E. Mackie in 1886 thanked Mr. R.F. Towndrow, who had given him very great help in making the list of flowers.

In 1872, Mr Towndrow contributed a series of papers on 'Butterflies and Moths' to the Natural History of the Malverns. His acute sense of observation was noticed during a joint party of the Worcestershire Club with the Malvern Field Club to Wyre Forest. The clubs met at Cleobury Mortimer, the birthplace of the Malvern Hills poet, William Langland, of 'Piers Plowman' fame. The report stated; 'The environs of the station had not been quitted before Mr. R.F. Towndrow, of the Malvern Club, found two specimens of habenaria bifolia (lesser butterfly orchis)'.

The diamond wedding of Mr and Mrs Towndrow was celebrated in 1929 when they received the following telegram from the private secretary to King George V and Queen Mary; 'I am commanded to convey to you both the hearty congratulations of the King and Queen on the happy occasion of your Diamond Wedding. Their Majesties trust that you may be spared to one another to enjoy the blessings of health and contentment for many years'.

Mrs Towndrow died three years later.

One of their five sons is living in Canada. There are 13 grandchildren and three great-grandchildren.

A member of Malvern Geographical Society and Malvern Higher Education Committee, Mr Towndrow had been one of the Managers of the Link Church School, and also the Warrington Church Schools, Malvern Wells.

He held an international honour as an Associate of the exclusive Linean Society, and had published three books containing a collection of poems.

Years ago he lectured to various societies in the locality and further afield. His first excursion with the Malvern Field Club, which he joined in 1846, took place in 1859, when he was 14 years old. Addressing the Club in 1899 the Rev. F.K. Clarke said he believed Mr Towndrow 'knew the habitat of every plant for miles around'."

Section 1

Reproduction from

'A Life, Love and other poems'

(Originally published 1889)

DEDICATION

O THOU, whose loving selfless life
Hath borne with mine in every mood,
Claim this, if there be aught of good,
For all of mine is thine, true wife.

PREFATORY NOTE TO "LOVE."

SOME word of explanation, or even of apology, seems called for in adopting a form of verse and an arrangement so intimately associated with our great Elegiac Poem, "In Memoriam."

A long and loving familiarity with that noble work: has shown the writer that in no other form could he, so agreeably to himself, find expression ; and therefore, at all risk, he ventures, in the spirit of admiration, to follow haltingly upon the path lying before him.

A LIFE

PART I - DEATH-IN-LIFE

MAD bells a-clashing from mossed tower merrily,
Pealing in joy, wildly, recklessly, free;
Showers of white roses, and crisp voices cheerily
Wishing good luck lo my darling and me.

Such was my dream. Did it reach to fruition?
How can I tell, for the days are long past?
How, when the truth seems less true than the vision,
Now that my soul is unclouded at last?

Still, as I try to recall the strange story,
Seems the far past and the present but one,
Faintly illumined with slow-dawning glory;
Veiled like the sun in the fulness of noon.

Yet I remember, th' awaked brain remembers,
Murmurs of water, a voice by the sea,
Seen through the mists of a score of Decembers
Glories of summer unfaded for me;

An autumnless summer': with winter succeeding
Close in the wake of its glory and glow;
An Eden of beauty, unwaning, unfading,
Passing at once to the dumbness of snow.

Sails a white crescent through blue deeps of heaven;
Sails a white crescent in blue deeps, ah me !
Scarce could we tell which was stiller that even,
The face of the sky or the face of the sea.

Voice by the water that reacheth me ever,
Low, with the lapping of waves on the shore:
Murmurs of eld that come faintly, but never
Change in their message to me any more.

Hush not twin voices nor heed the commotion,
Heed not the changes of time and of sea,
Hush not sad voices, from lips and from ocean,
Still through the distance speak ever to me !

I low like a portrait some master has painted,
Seen through the smoke and the dimness of years,
Looketh a face from the shadow untainted,
Chastened in beauty by sorrow and tears !

Fade not, sweet face, if a dream yet be lasting;
Wane not, sad face, with thy mem'ries sublime;
Thou, with thy mem'ries and sorrows unwasting,
Look out for aye from the canvas of time.

Bright days a-passing but each tinged with sorrow,
Sorrow mysterious that no man may tell,
Wild fears of something awaiting the morrow,
Soon in its turn to bear yesterday's spell.

Light, softly saddened, through white curtains stealing,
Touching the face of my saint in her sleep ;
Worth, to unworth, in its beauty revealing,
Bearing on moon-beams a call from the deep.

Ye who would tell of the canonized many,
Write ye Saint Ellen among your white names !
Write her as one fair and spotless as any
Lighted to rest by Domitian's flames.

Fair virgin spirit, how clean thou appearest ;
Starlight to vapour thou seemest to mine
Sadly I know that thy nearest, thy dearest,
Showest all black by that whiteness of thine.

Low roll and murmur of water receding,
Slow-moving rhythm it soundeth to me;
Undertone plaintive of passionless pleading,
Broken again by a call from the sea.

Pure are the blue walls the silent moon clambers;
Pure the still earth where her white currents flow;
Could they but wash through my soul's dismal chambers
Then were they fairer? but how can I know ?

How can I know? there are clear voices falling,
Borne through the night on the moonlight to me,
Sweetly they call me; again, 'tis the falling,
Tear-like, of whispers that come from the sea.

Fair face thou seemest all-haloed with glory,
How shall I dare to remain at thy side?
Seek I the shore, where the ocean's edge hoary
Turns on the sand, and grow worthy my bride.

Flame-whitened fingers that trace out our story,
Mystical letters on tablet of sky
(Ah! could we read them!) unveil your weird glory,
Spell out the doom that I know draweth nigh.

Fair moon from white web of vapour escaping,
Look on a soul in the black web of sin,
Ceaselessly ever in agony, shaping
Forms from the chaos of vision within.

Rolling of waters and coldness of ocean ;
Rolling of cloud-waves and coldness of sky;
Rolling of brain in its tortured emotion ;
Coldness of limbs-of heart-soul-and I die.

Die—why not die? Strangely folk talk of dying,
Meaning we pass from *that* life into *this*;
Die from the frenzy, the anguish, the sighing,
Live to beatitude, .silence, and bliss.

PART II. - LIFE-IN-DEATH

STILL, sweetly still, no longer wild storms vex,
Nor any more
The driven soul, safe-moored, hath fear of wrecks
On this sweet shore.

Is't life or death? Life past all dread of death,
Beyond the roll
Of voices, scarce the wafting of a breath
From soul to soul.

Mountains behind us, bearing each a crown
Like frosted ore,
And shedding silver tears, that trickle down
And reach the shore.

Th' eternal sea before us, in the light
Of early sun
Shadow and reflex of the hills, by night,
Glory of moon.

A silent sea, whose soft lips ever press
The silent sand,
Eternal, changeless, love, one long caress
Of sea and land.

Calm mountains, conscious of their glory, swathed
In ferny sheen
And steeped in sunlight, burning not, but bathed
In living green;

Clear rippling golden sun-waves passing through
The feath'ry forms,
Gemmed opalescent, with undrying dew
And tears of storms,—

Storms such as lash the earth but may not break
Our sacred sleep,
Yet rolling o'er us, in their weakness shake
And feebly weep.

Low clouds, like incense, float beneath the trees
And fall and rise,
And bear their dower of whispered messages
From yearning skies.

Here rest we, where across our pleasant land
No sorrows fall,
To me 'tis just the hollow of His hand
Who orders all.

And sometimes, in those folded mists that pass
In solemn grace,
I see, but dimly, as in darkened glass,
A sweet sad face :

But yesterday—I think 'twas yesterday—
It came not sad,
Sweet as of old, with sorrow passed away,
Not wholly glad,

But calm, with calmness most divine and fair,
Nor pale, nor wan ;
A face, like one that sleepeth in the air
With moon-beams on

In tender touches; all the hair suffused
With glory-beams ;
As long ago, a sweet fair face was used
To come in dreams :

In dreams, strange dreams, and always with the roll
Of summer seas,
And white moon looking down like sainted soul
And guarding these,

And ever passing on her noiseless way
Through wondering stars,
Night's queen and bride, whose locks about her lay
In silver bars.

So came it here to me : the same sweet face,
And not the same,
Then sweet and sad : now sweet and girt with grace
Of gentlest flame.

Slow wanes the day and glideth on the flight
I hold so dear ;
It cometh softly, perhaps the blessed sight
Is drawing near.

* * * * *

O folded cloud, unfold ; I know thou hast
A treasure there!
O folded cloud, thou hearest from the vast
My vision fair!

O weird white rolling cloud, o'ershadow me,
Thy white wings lift;
Unveil thy heart of hearts that I may see
The precious gift

* * * *

The same sweet face ; the same calm eyes, the same
All but the woe,
Their tears, now priceless pearls, in that clear flame
That orbs them, glow.

My dream, my dream, again: my soul is thrilled
With blest surprise,
And fain would question of the woe that filled,
Of old, those eyes.

But they divine the words my awe-hushed breath
Still fails to give,
And falls the answer, "This is life, not death,
I died to live."

O rolling cloud in incense-smoke expire,
Where lieth deep
The mountain's shadow, thou hast roused desire
From dreamless sleep.

Faint, floating memories reach me, as thy breath
That sweepeth past,
And beareth tokens of the living death
To deathless vast.

So, ever death-in-life shall yearn to see
Our living land,
And grasp the skirts of immortality
With faltering hand.

Still, sweetly still, no longer tempests come,
But mystic forms
Float vapour-borne across our silent home,
Devoid of storms.

O mountains, wide your arms protecting spread,
And thou, O sea,
Complete the circle of our blest and dread
Security!

PART III. - THE AWAKENING

I.

FADED, all faded, gone the ore-crowned hills ;
The mute and still illimitable sea,
And hushed the murmur of the distant rills
That promised music through eternity !
All faded, faded, e'en the mists are riven
And hang like tattered robes against the sky,
And wrecked the home of rest, the silent heaven,
Where I had thought for evermore to lie !
I dreamed I dreamed, and in that inner dream
I saw all things fade from me, then I woke,
And all was as before, no shadow-stroke
Nor touch of dimness on the lightest beam.
But I am truly wakened now and see
That inner dream and this are truth to me.

2.

Where is the face that came to me in sleep,
In that strange restful sleep I fancied death,
Within the inmost circle of the deep
That, closing, stilled the nigh-suspended breath?
Sweet face where art thou? Lo! thou earnest first
In that old life, so beautiful, so sad,
With soft soul-music; then they whispered, "Mad,"
And thou reflectedst all thou deem'dst of worst:
Again, thou earnest in the silent home
Wearing a chastened loveliness of woe,
And heaven-born pity ever with thee came;
And, once again, all girt with silver flame,
And from thy lips the clear-toned cherished flow,
Like sweet bird-carols when the morn has come.

3.

Speak once again sweet voice from out the cloud!
Voice from that world of stillness speak to me!
O sweet low voice not ever silent be,
If thou canst bring no comfort, then, speak loud
In rushing torrent! Though the waters be
But bitter let me thirst not utterly!
O form, as dear as voice, how once ye shone
From out the stooping cloud and then wert lost,
Yet left behind a light (as meteor tost
Through blackness leaves its milky pathway shown
As witness on the wondering face of night);
But now 'tis faded, those dear lips have ceased
To utter comfort "to a mind diseased,"
That yearns to breast the nearing flood of light.

4.

New men, new faces, with a ceaseless hum
Of unfamiliar voices on mine ear,
At distance seeming, and yet uttered near,
Strange and unmeaning unto me they come ;
And I reply but vaguely, or am dumb,
Or, when I know the burden, answer make
Of such small things as constitute the sum
Of those small lives that on the silence break.
One voice, albeit in whispers, would be heard
Across the gulf of space, but that is still,
And though I hearken for the lightest word
It cometh not. And everyday the hill
Its shadows gathers, like a mighty pall,
And lifeless sunbeams on the ocean fall.

5.

Lo, I have seen a face so like to thine,
Can he who drew it e'er have looked on thee ?
A face so full of sympathy divine,
And shadowing forth a true soul's agony;
An utter self-forgetfulness of woe,
And mute with inexpressible despair,
Yet with such loveliness beyond compare,
In that soul-beauty, as the angels know.
The master saw thee where the ivied wall
Nor hid thy shadowed beauty, nor betrayed
Where watchful leaves in tender touches played
And wove their veil of mystery over all.
And oh, how like that ivy's help is this,
Which thou hast given from out thy feebleness.

6.

"Dead, and we dare not tell him," so the breath
Of men is borne me, while one whispers low,
"The world is poorer, having lost her worth."
Spake she not truly, "This is life, not death"?
And know I not her fealty?—ah, I know
That she were with me if at all on earth.
Friends, I beseech you, if ye pity me,
Lead me where ye have laid her. I am past
All passion, like a spent and broken blast
That once wrought wreck but now moans helplessly.
One said "her worth," but where is any one
Who knew it as I knew it ? See, I bring
My poor tear-tribute for an offering
To greet your kindness. Leave me here alone.

7.

"Lo, here thou liest, and I lay my head
Beside thee, as of old, upon the grass
And thou art silent ; clear bell-voices pass
From yon grey tower, and reach us, and the dead
Alone are watchers with my love and me.
From morn till noon the shadow of the tree
Falls lightly on thee, and at eve the tower's
Cool shade steals out to this still home of ours,
(For any spot is home that holdeth thee,
In precious keeping, till all shadows flee) :—
Speak, dearest, once, from out thy blessed state:"
So spake I; then an answer fell, as light
As snowflake falling through a silent night
On face uplifted, this was all, "I wait."

8.

"The world is poorer, having lost her worth;"
The world is richer having known her love;
And I, with footsteps ever swifter, move
Through lessening distance to that other birth,
Which men call death, the nearing gate of life.
"Move on to death and silence," thus, they say;
"Move on to living converse," I reply,
"To those calm voices past the hum of strife;
To scorchless sun-waves where no shadows stray;
To living forms that have no thought to die."
The earth is richer. Where the sunbeam falls
The fruits are riper, flowers more richly bright,
Nor lose their beauty when the loving light
Is drawn again within the golden halls.

9.

The old grey tower! again my early dream
And here, where flowers fell, a flower lies
More fair than aught were scattered; still the skies
Above us bend, as then, with summer gleam.
I speak, I look, upon the past as though
Once more 'twere present, and in fancy seem
To lose the margins of Life's narrow stream
And make a sea of Time, whose waters show
A sheen of glory hiding gulfs of gloom.
But, from the mystery of that awful deep,
A voice no more a whisper of the tomb,
But like a voice that stilleth them that weep,
Comes ever to me now, in accents great
With comfort, this is all, "I wait; I wait."

10.

Thou art not, dear, so very far from me;
Thou seemest nearer than thou wert the day
Thou spakest to me in the quiet home :
And may I not a little closer come
In sweet soul-converse? May I hear thee say,
"Thou nearest ever as the shadows flee
Before the daybreak that thou knowest of"?
So would I hear thee speak—if that might be
Yet am I well contented with thy love
That faileth not, as I draw nigh to thee.
So pass the months of waiting since that day
When, once again, the tumult silence broke
With loveless discord, and my Sorrow woke
To know herself—and while the time away.

11.

Say, have I not communion with thy soul
Across the deep of space—to thee no space
Nor any deep at all? Have I not felt
The evening breathings on my forehead melt
And known them for thy kisses? From thy place
Hast thou not given some earnest of that whole
I would know fully? Thou wert with me, dear,
In that first whirl of passion; then again
In sweetest dream I often knew thee near;
And now I need thee most—in aching pain
Of loneliness elsewise—I feel thee here,
And dearer to my soul than summer rain.
So help me ever with that love of thine
Across the years till it be one with mine.

PART IV. - HOPE

1.

WHITE-ROBED, star-crowned, shining Three,
  Bending o'er the silent dead,
Faith and Hope and Charity,
  Lead me where I would be led !

God-born maidens given to man,
  Spirit-brides to all who list,
Scattering clouds that veil His plan,
  Lighting beacons in the mist.

Star-browed maiden, clear-eyed Faith,
  Counting not the feeble hours ;
Ever, from the dust of Death,
  Seeing blossom living flowers.

Thou, who, past the gloom, canst see
  Distant lights to which we grope
Through the darkness trustfully,
  Star-browed maiden, radiant Hope.

Thou, whose power nor great nor small
  Knoweth to its full degree—
Hoping all, enduring all—
  Star-browed maiden, Charity.

Ye who, like Orion's zone,
  Shine from heaven, O starry Three,
Dwell with me, as ye were one,
  Faith and Hope and Charity.

2.

With weary wings,
Tired dove, thou seekest rest in vain,
In fruitless wanderings,
Between the arched sky and watery plain:
Lone dove, lone dove,
No rest for thee but with thy waiting love.

No rest for thee ;
No feathered crest of mountain wood
Canst thou at distance see
'Twixt cloudless sky and waste of shoreless flood :
Lone dove lone dove,
One waiteth still to welcome back thy love.

No rest on earth :
Beat high, true heart, for thou art come
To where a hand put forth
Will take thee, tired-winged wanderer, back to home :
Lone dove, lone dove,
Lone dove no longer, thou hast found thy love.

Tired soul of mine,
Blank sky above, beneath thee earth,
Where sunbeams never shine
With those old glories that they once put forth :
O weary soul
No rest till thou hast reached the nearing goal.

Beneath the tree
Thou hoverest—bird of ravished nest—
Moaning continually
And finding not, yet drawing near to rest :
O weary soul
Thou hearest still the surging time-waves roll.

Twixt light and dark
Thou waitest—joy ! thou yet shalt win
Thy rest, when from His ark
God's hand put forth shall take thee, tired one, in,
And, O glad soul !
Thy broken joys shall be again made whole.

3.

The face of my love like an angel came
   Silently down the night,
Haloed about with a silver flame
   Filling her tresses with light.

A look and a smile, and her soul was poured
   Deep into mine as I lay,
As the light of love, in her sweet eyes stored,
   Awoke like the birth of day.

Then I spread my arms through the empty night,
  As sweet sleep slid down from above,*
And I knew, when I waked in the dawning light,
  My spirit had met its love.

4.

The world was white,
A little snowdrop reared its snowy head :
The world grew dark, it sunk within its bed
Away from sight:

It lieth low,
And gathers beauty, till again the earth
Is pure enough to usher in its birth
With robe of snow.

The world seemed white,
A snowdrop that I knew her head uprose :
The world grew dark, she sought again repose
Beyond out sight:

But blossometh,
With fadeless beauty, where the angels see,
In that white world,* her spotless purity,
Which knows not death.

* "The gentle sleep from Heaven
That *slid* into my soul."
(Rime of the Ancient Mariner.)

5.

A voice from out the gathered years
  Proclaimeth, while One lays them by,
With comfort, "They that sow in tears
  Shall reap" (O harvest blest !) "in joy."

O harvest rich with precious fruit;
  O comfort, though our hearts will bleed,
O heavenly flowers from earthly root
  Where we have sown the bitter seed !

O comfort thou art near akin
  To sorrow; thy true hand is laid,
With whispers to the deeps within,
  Most gently on the lowest head.

* "White World" a beautiful Welsh term for Heaven.

6.

Little child that playest here,
  Where the yew's dark shadow waves,
Little child, without a fear
  Playing in among the graves.

Bring your dolls and bring your toys,
  Come and sit beneath the tree,
For to you belong the joys,
  As the sorrows unto me.

We are playmates dear and true,
  So we must our secrets share,
Very old am I to you,
  You to me are very fair.

Lapt in shadow near us lies
  One I love in slumber deep,
But she heareth not the noise,
  For she lies so sound asleep.

Child, I think when she was young
  She was even such as you ;
With a little prattling tongue,
  And a little love as true.

Child, God grant that when the bells
  Clash for you so wildly free,
You may prove to some one else
  What my darling was to me.

We were playmates, little one,
  But she had a sorrow deep,
So they laid her softly down
  Till she cried herself to sleep;

Sleep that wakes not till the dawn
  Break at last in morning clear,
But the evening draweth on
  When I sleep to wake with her.

7.

Brooklet, with a ceaseless song,
  Sadly sweet its melody,
Bearing one poor leaf along
  Swiftly, surely, tremblingly.

Withered leaf that would not stay,
  Nor the lily blossoms see,
Since a flower was plucked away
  That was blooming close to thee.

Thou O brook, with every hour
  Bear along thy leaf with thee
Till it find again the flower
  In the bosom of the sea.

8.

Belovèd mine,
Waiting and watching from the closed gate
I know thee, while I hear the loved "I wait"
From lips of thine.

True spirit blest,
On Time's stream thou a withered leaf canst see
That nears the ocean of Eternity
Where thou hast rest.

Across the years
(As steals a mother's hand), from out the cloud,
Thy promise finds me when my head is bowed,
And dries my tears.

I know that thou,
By that old truth told once in those dear eyes,
Beside the trysting-gate of Paradise
Art waiting now.

Beneath the hum
Of voices thy clear whisper reaches me
With comfort, while I fain would answer thee
To thy blest home
With rapture—but the night is drawing late,
I pause and listen for the opening gate
To greet its sound, and, to thy loved "I wait,"
Reply, "I come."

LOVE

TO LOVE. (1 COR. XIII. 13.)

LAST of the Three yet first of all;
  Thou comprehendest Hope and Faith ;
  Thou livest past the death of Death,
And blossomest when blossoms fall.

Eternal Love, thou comest here
  With heavenly light upon thy wings ;
  Thou movest 'midst familiar things,
That catch thy gleams when thou art near.

All meanest gifts to gold are turned
  By thy sweet presence ; graces meet
  And lie like flowers about thy feet,
Homely and poor, by thee unspurned.

All natures yield-the worst, the best
  To thy most subtle alchemy,
  The noble from the base, and free
Themselves from self, at thy behest.

Though overweighted, dragged in dirt,
  Thy whiteness reasserts its hue ;
  Thou, if not scathless, passest through
All wrestling with no mortal hurt.

Nay, more, thy foes, in falling, bless
  Thy power of victory, as they feel
  Thy contact strengthens; bruises heal;
And conquests end in blessedness.

Wounded within thy friend's house, still
  Undaunted, thou, for their behoof,
  Yet tarriest till their niggard roof
Is blest by that it counted ill.

And this to these who scorn thee ! what
  To those who fullest welcome give,
  Who living love, and loving live,
Nor deem it life where thou art not:

Souls that have felt the angel's touch;
  Souls that a Presence oft has stirred ;
  Souls that, perchance, have sinned yet heard
"Forgiven, for they loved much :"

O what to these? A larger share
  (To him that hath shall still be given) :
  A glimpse of heaven still opens heaven,
And longing almost takes us there.

O highest grace, all gifts above,
  When from the heights that none may see,
  God issued in humility
And took thy name and came as Love.

Last, greatest, of the glorious Three,
  Thy warmth and light to me be sent,
  That words, not wholly impotent,
Full of thyself may rise to thee.

I.
LOVE'S ONENESS.

The love of "man and bird and beast,"
  Though varied in its onward course,
  And in degree, has common source—
The greatest but a greater least.

From one deep fount, one shoreless sea
  (Before, no death; behind, no birth),
  Whence all returns, it issues forth—
The bosom of Immensity.

II.
RESPONSIBILITY.

MAN, dwelling here with beast and bird,
  And working wreck with lesser loves
  By stronger will, unconscious moves
Beneath a heaven where all are heard.

He, dumb creation's head and priest,
  Should he, alas ! himself be dumb
  And blind and deaf what sorrows come
What joys are lost, to great and least.

He lives not to himself nor dies
  Unto himself, he causeth moan
  Or waketh gladness, not alone
He walks beneath impartial skies :

To him is turned imploring eye,
  Beseeching gesture, voiceless speech
  Of cringing attitude, that reach,
Too often, but his vanity.

"He prayeth best who loveth best;"
  Ah ! truth, this power of loving grows
  To power of prayer, and he who knows
To love, knows best where love may rest.

III.
THE MEASURE.

Perchance the stature of the man,
  In Eyes that see not as we see,
  Is just his love's capacity
The standard of a nobler plan.

Perchance the muscle or the will;
  The subtle brain ; the steady arm ;
  The beauty seen in face or form ;
The cunning fingers' rapid skill ;

The gift to plan a perfect whole;
  The grasp of small or great events,
  Are only love's embellishments—
Soul-garments, lacking still the soul.

Who knows, a loving child may be,
  In yonder world where all is clear,
  Seen greater than the loveless seer,
Who here seemed nigh a deity !

Who knows? Who knows? Where much is hidden,
  This truth, I think, is plain at least,
  The loveless soul, at Love's high feast,
Will be the marriage guest unbidden.

IV.
LOVE'S SYMBOL.

Is love from form inseparate?
  May not the soul be truly loved
  For its own self, that we are moved
So deeply by its outward state?

We seem to love but what we see;
  Can this be so? or is the form
  The symbol only of a charm
Too deeply placed for scrutiny?

What priceless beauty may we find,
  To us alone revealed and given,
  As gazers on the lower heaven
Know yet the heaven of heavens behind.

None other may the secret share;
  Ours is the sign, the countersign
  (Where "mine" is "thine," and "thine" is "mine"),
And love's low speech falls everywhere.

For us, the hidden force that dwells
  Within, by mystic influence
  Transfers its likeness to the sense,
As fair sea-creatures fashion shells.

V.
LOVE'S IDEAL.

I deem the perfect pattern whole
  Is never seen in one on earth;
  That two must fuse their separate worth,
And soul complete its fellow-soul.

I deem no life, since His alone,
  The Type of all, to us was sent,
  But needs its proper complement
To round it to the perfect one.

No life save His, whose mighty plan,
  Before our wistful, doubting eyes,
  Portrays love's possibilities—
Type of the woman and the man.

Life unapproachable ! Yet we
  May gaze on that we cannot reach,
  While unto all, and unto each,
The charge is ever, "Follow Me!"

Yet sometimes our experience yields
  A glimpse of one (O vision sweet)
  Who sees the footprints of those feet,
And follows through these lower fields :

Ah, not for us to say how far;
  HE only, who unfaltering trod
  The pathway to the mount of God,
Knows what its fiery trials are.

VI.
MOTHS.

Does that desire which ends in shame,
  To love unconscious tribute pay,
  As moths that shun the light of day
Seek yet the light of candle-flame?

O shrivelled wings, and blinded sight;
  O what a gain and loss is this;
  O what a travesty of bliss,
To find the flame and lose the light.

VII.
EARTH-BOUND.

I know the thoughtless often call
  A lower passion by a name
  We honour so, and gather shame
For that they scarcely know at all.

Poor hapless ones in piteous case,
  Whose highest is a thing so low ;
  Who never see the mountain's brow,
Above the clouds that wrap its base.

For them no distant peak exists;
  No spotless crown of virgin snow,
  That takes the glory and the glow
From highest height beyond the mists.

Shall these no dream nor mother's love
  Lift, where the sullen fog-clouds tost
  Conceal no more the blessing lost;
The good they have no memory of?

VIII.
SHADOWS.

Despair and darkness, death and doubt,
  All cast their gloom across the skies,
  And, from our feeble, faithless eyes,
Shut Heaven's sweet light and glory out.

The light, still there, to us no more
  Asserts its old supremacy;
  What once we saw we cannot see,
Though God is where He was before.*

The light still there : the shadow here :
  But who may leave the jealous gloom;
  Who quit the chamber of the tomb,
When Life and Love have left him there?

Bound hand and foot with grave-clothes : night
  About him in the silent earth,
  Until the Lord-of-Love's "Come forth!"
Shall call again to life and light.

* "But think that God ys ther He was." — JOHN LYDGATE.

IX.
TYPES.

Three gifts, of light, of life, and love,
  All symbolize, in their degree,
  The Source of all, and surely we
May through them see His Spirit move.

The light which floods the earth and sky;
  The "Light which lighteth every man,"
  Proclaim the unity of plan,
The oneness in diversity.

Life, which all nature permeates
  In ceaseless flow, whose source we deem
  With Thee, the Life, the Fount, the Stream,
From whence all being emanates.

That gift of love whose crowning bliss,
  Whose most divine beatitude,
  Is not its own, but other's good,
And stores its sweetness up for this.

Light, life, and love, Thy gifts we see
  (But Thou art greater than them all),
  Who hearest when we yearning call
For something that will show us Thee.

X.
"WHAT REWARD HAVE YE?"

"What if this excellence you crave,
  A dream of love, with life should end,
  And this brief pathway only tend
Through darkness to a senseless grave?

"What if this insubstantial dream
  Be but a thing of days and hours,
  With gladness as of summer flowers;
Or flies, that sport above the stream

"Through some small fragment of a day
  On gauzy wings, while underneath
  Sweeps ever on the tide of death,
Alike unheeding toil or play?

"A hundred years, and where will be
  This love of thine, this rapture high?
  The green of earth, and blue of sky,
Will gladden those who follow thee.

"Why struggle? What can fruitless strife
  With evil, prudish joys, avail?
  I count that fair is one with frail,
And counsel drain the wine of life."

As sudden clouds in spring-time come
  And touch some fair sun-lighted hill
  With shadow, and the air grows chill,
These whispers reach me-I am dumb.

As sunbeams, with undaunted strength,
  Some fissure find in gathered gloom,
  And flood the hill and fill the room,
My heart's true answer comes at length.

" 'What if this dream should end in dust?'
  Such is your burden, even then
  'Twere surely best to die as men,
As lords of self, than slaves of lust.

" 'Love ends with life.' I yield, but here
  Agreement ceases : God's own breath
  And highest grace know naught of death
In passing to a higher sphere.

"I count that nothing good and pure
  (As nothing evil) lives unfelt,
  And, when a hundred ages melt,
The impress of a love is sure.

" 'A hundred years;' this life, this love,
  Will still be young. Eternal truth
  Dwells always in eternal youth,
Albeit a hundred aeons move.

"O better blank and sightless eyes;
  And better death (if that might be),
  Than sight which can but frailty see
In that last gift of Paradise.

"Thy counsel? Yes, the hours go past,
  And nears the time of setting sun
  When we may take the cup from One
Who keeps His good wine till the last."

XI.
LOVE'S INFLUENCES.

"Like rain upon the mown grass," so,
  In times of weakness or distress,
  My love's love comes with power to bless,
And all the phantoms rise and go.

So, when those gentle whispers come,
  And, through the war of tongues, speak peace,
  For me all other voices cease,
And Discord's clanging words are dumb.

One touch, but one, has power to move
  When this poor heart is beating low,
  A touch that it alone can know—
The sympathy of love with love.

XII.
DEATH AND FAITH.

Death, thou art not of life the end,
  Nor its beginning; through thy gate
  We pass but to a fuller state,
To which unwilling footsteps tend !

Death, thou art not the end of love,
  Nor love's beginning; thy sharp frost
  May ripen, at an awful cost,
The fruit we were so slow to prove !

Death, thou dost limit set to sight,
  And, in thy garment's pierceless fold,
  Our dearest dust relentless hold
In seeming dawnless, endless, night!

Death, thou art victor till our faith
  Itself asserts, nor helpless waits,
  But storms with force and fire thy gates,
And lights with love the halls of death!

XIII.
LOVE'S PRISONER.

Whatever depths of black despair
  Engulf me, yet, 'tis all to know
  I cannot ever sink below
The arms of Love beneath me there.

Whatever heights it may be given
  My soul to reach past earthly things,
  I cannot leave Love's guarding wings—
The boundless boundaries of heaven.

I cannot lay my head in sleep—
  In sleep or in that deeper rest—
  But I am pillowed on the breast
That stilleth all the souls that weep.

I cannot live without Love's breath,
  And, in the fields of Paradise
  We hope to tread, those dewy eyes
Will greet me through the gate of Death.

So, always, everywhere I move
  I bounded am by Love's decree—
  A prisoner girt about with sea—
I cannot quit the realm of Love.

XIV.
LOVE'S PHASES.

Love manifest is multiform,
  And looking on some lovely phase
  Whose sweetness gladdens sombre days,
Like sun gleam after sullen storm,

We fancy we have seen the goal
  Of human love and pure desire,
  Unconscious of a summit higher,
Still rising from the perfect whole.

What tender touch, what reverent breath,
  Can make the Jove of mother known?
  To all the line of mothers shown
In that sweet type at Nazareth,

To which, we also love to know,
  A Type of childhood too was given
  In tender Love that came from heaven,
And showed us all must enter so.

The love of husband, love of wife;
  And those that look to these as crown;
  And fainter touches, running down
To children's early dream of life.

The love of father, here the sign
  Of that Eternal Fatherhood
  Whose every gift and every good
In one stupendous Good combine.

And hers, the sister's (strong and weak),
  A brother's keeper, in the power
  She gathers, in some quiet hour,
From strength she knows so well to seek.

And that deep brother-love, whose doubt
  Yet sees, in love on him bestowed,
  Some light that on a treacherous road
He surely yet will follow out.

The love of friends ; adown the years
  How, all undimmed, the story runs
  Of Saul's and Jesse's noble sons
Who sealed their compact with their tears.

And hers, that other love outpoured
  (That hath a promise all its own
  Of being known where He is known),
The woman's for her sinless Lord.

So, from that mighty Heart of Love
  All streams, of varied force and powers,
  Flow out, and so prepare the hours
For that great day to which we move.

XV.
LOVE'S COMPENSATION.

The mother whom we often see
  With trouble worn, and bearing trace
  Of care upon her furrowed face,
And doomed, we think, to drudgery,

Has yet some secret source of joy;
  Some hidden mine in which she still
  Finds compensation for her ill;
Some gold, nor heeds the gold's alloy.

Perchance with husband weak and poor,
  And hearty children, guessing not
  (Blest ignorance) how hard her lot
To fight the wolf about the door :

Yet would she not go back again
  To less of love and more of ease,
  She sees what none beside her sees,
And sets her good above her pain.

O could we look on her aright,
  Her plainness would to beauty grow,
  And sweet self-sacrifice would show
Her lines of care as lines of light.

XVI.
LOVE'S SECRET.

That life which seems to walk alone,
  Or take a simple interest
  In trivial matters at the best,
And looks a mystery to none;

Whose smile the little children seek,
  And bring their troubles to an ear
  That never grudges time to hear
Because the tale is long or weak :

And sometimes, when a thoughtful mood
  Arrests her little prattlers,
  They wonder why a life like hers
Is largely spent in solitude :

Why no one else has found the charm ;
  No nearer life has shared the love,
  That moves where'er her footsteps move,
So self-contained, so sweet, so warm.

O little ones, your little powers
  Can never guess, till you too know
  The vestal flame that burns below,
So steadfast, through the silent hours.

O hidden fire, your heat pervades
  All nature, like the generous sun
  That blesses all he looks upon
With influence fadeless though he fades.

That life, that we have thought alone,
  Within itself a love enfolds
  That ever sweetest converse holds
With love, the reflex of its own.

Those loves know naught of time or space;
  Those loves have bridged Death's chasm o'er,
  And, from the near and further shore,
They meet in spirit face to face.

XVII.
THE FLOOD.

How all love points in its degree
  To that great passion, virtue, grace,
  That dim-seen vision of the Face
That one day we may bear to see.

A rill of revelation here,
  And there some stronger currents gleam
  From that expanse of love, whose stream
Is bounded by the banks we rear.

Not always. Sometimes bound and bank
  Are swept away, all barriers bow
  Before the ceaseless mighty flow
Whose waters once we lightly drank,

And thought perhaps in happy mood
  (The draught was sweet as pleasant dream)
  That we were greater than the stream,
And nothing guessed of power or flood :

And while we mused or idly slept,
  Ere yet a heart was lost or won,
  The flood was coming grandly on
And silently about us crept,

And all our force of will was gone,
  As, waking in an ecstasy,
  We knew the stream was more than we,
And hailed the flood that bore us on.

XVIII.
LOVE'S GROWTH.

How scorching heat or chilling frost
  Will ripen love; the fiery breath
  Of evil missed or shade of death
May show us what we might have lost.

And in an hour the growth of years,
  Well-nigh unheeded by our eyes,
  Attains its sweetness, and we prize
The bloom and beauty that it wears.

We take the gift, like that of air,
  As ours by right, till sudden blows
  A stronger breath which sternly shows
A force without us stirring there.

Or, like that other dower of health,
  Which he who has it scarcely feels
  Until some failing power reveals
The priceless treasure of his wealth.

A touch, a simple word, a glance,
  May stir the core of latent fire
  To leaping flame, and bring desire
For vaster sphere of circumstance.

The old routine may seem the same ;
  No sign to others of a light,
  Now brightest on the starless night—
A hidden, quenchless, vestal flame.

And may it be to others given,
  Who know not here the depths, the heights,
  That love may trim its feeble lights
To brightness in the halls of heaven?

XIX.
EVENING.

When at the threshold of the night
  I walk alone in summer fields,
  And every flower its perfume yields
As offering to departing light,

A weird, mysterious, sense of awe,
  I know not in the deeper gloom,
  Creeps over me, with touch of doom,
Before the universal law.

Sleep, darkness, death, and in their train
  The waking, and the life and light,
  Until we see the blessed sight
And these no more come back again.

XX.
FROM DARK TO LIGHT.

How vast all nature seems at night,
  When our near view of earth is lost
  In shadow, and the great suns tost,
Through darkness, show themselves in light.

When gazing into ether far,
  We leave the near and follow fast
  With thought and vision to the vast,
Where plunges some receding star.

All things recede ; all fly the face
  Upturned, and O how well he knows,
  The watcher, of the light that grows
Intenser in a deep'ning space.

Shall it be so when shadows fall
  Before that great Epiphany;
  That following on the light we see
We find at last the Light of all?

XXI.
LIFE'S VICTORY.

I thought if only Death were dead,
  If he, whom all men bow before,
  Were stricken prone, with power no more
To blanch the cheek and lay the head—

If he no more were king and lord,
  Who works his will on man and beast,
  Who sat in type at ancient feast,
Or hung an ill-suspended sword—

If only lie were buried deep
  Beside his victims, what a load
  Would fall, where yonder shadowed road
To trembling feet grows rough and steep.

If we might dream of permanence
  For aught we do, what added zest
  Would make our best a better best,
Sure-founded on experience.

Yet Death is more than dead, he lives
  A slave, where once he held his state,
  A porter at Life's awful gate,
Who entrance to his victims gives.

XXII.
NEW LIFE.

Suppose a man from out the night
  And ashes of an ancient tomb,
  In some deep-buried city's gloom,
Should pass at once to upper light;

Suppose that such an one had made
  The tomb his chamber; long had dwelt
  With blackness, such as might be felt,
Upon him like a garment laid,

Whose folds about his senses drawn
  Had numbed his will, and every ray
  Of past experience shut away—
With Hope long dead and Memory gone.

If such a man, whose doubt and dread
  Had perished in the realm of use,
  Not dreaming he had aught to lose,
Or aught to gain-alive or dead—

If he at length his hand should lay,
  As oftentimes in days before,
  On that blank wall and find a door,
And sudden issue into day,

And all his better past return ;
  And Hope arise from death and live;
  And birds again their carols give;
And old affections rise and burn:

Would not a vision so unguessed,
  Unhoped for, seem a thing so high
  He dare not grasp it, but would lie
In trembling rapture, blest-unblest—

And, blind with light and faint with love,
  Receive in awe the gracious streams;
  As from his night of hideous dreams
He feels the daybreak o'er him move.

XXIII.
IF LOVE WERE NOT?

What if the springs of love should cease,
  And life be loveless ; human eyes
  Gleam cold as February skies,
And blankness take the place of peace?

I think the birds would cease to sing;
  And fairest flowers forget to blow;
  And all the weight of helpless woe
Be borne by every living thing.

What if the springs of love should cease,
  And man become a loveless soul;
  Whose visions high should rend, and roll
In one dull round of seeming peace ?

This were true death, if love were lost ;
  The silence of a stringless lyre;
  A dead earth, with no heart of fire,
In outer and in inner frost.

Then all were silent, all at rest—
  Th' unruffled rest that smoothes the face,
  And binds the waters in their place,
And stills the wild lake's heaving breast.

This were no peace-this stillness sealed ;
  This were no sleep—this lack of breath :
  No peace; no sleep—but victor Death
Upon his silent battle-field.

XXIV.
SUNSET.

I saw the heavens aflame with light
  Of sunset; lakes of opal green,
  With golden shores, and all between
Vast tracts of purple, rosy-bright;

And deeper hues and points of gold,
  And glowing slopes, and liquid fire,
  And peaks of unattained desire,
And hollow haunts of light untold;

And scattered broadcast o'er the sky,
  Soft fragments from some golden fleece;
  And all the sight was one of peace—
The peace of silent ecstasy.

And, somewhere, was a mighty heart
  Of light, a hidden core of heat,
  From whence the fervent glories beat
And flowed with fire to every part.

A sense of latent power was there,
  Calm, unimpassioned, full of rest,
  In its self-knowledge knowing best
The force that minor forces share.

A vision shown and then withdrawn
  Within the folds of Day's eclipse;
  An awful sweet apocalypse
Of one eternal, deathless dawn.

XXV.
SUNSET DREAMS.

Another vision comes to me—
  All nature fills, all thought pervades—
  Reveals itself, withdraws, and fades
Again into obscurity.

Now all creation palpitates
  With throbbing life, which often seems
  To seek again the home of dreams,
That lies within the viewless gates :

Those gates that open now and then,
  To some, we trust, in time of doubt,
  To whom the glory pouring out
Is as a stream to thirsting men.

And some there are who having seen
  (Like Arthur's knights who saw the Grail),
  Feel darkness now can naught avail
To hide a sign that once hath been :

To them the glimpse, a moment given,
  Itself surpasses, and the sight
  Is but the herald of the light
Beyond these threshold lamps of heaven :

To them the life and light, that move
  In earth and heaven and distant star,
  Are but the beatings from afar
Of that great Heart we name as Love.

XXVI.
THE NEAR AND THE FAR.

One sang of Laura praise that stirs
  Time's echoes; one of Beatrice
  A vision showed beyond all price,
Inspired by that sweet soul of hers.

That story dear to school-boy days
  (When self-less love such welcome has),
  Of Damon and of Pythias,
Still wins from us its meed of praise.

Such love, I doubt not, still is given,
  Above the light of lurid days;
  But, standing near a beacon's blaze,
We scarce discern the lamps of heaven.

XXVII.
THE SMALL AND THE GREAT.

How often trifles vex the soul,
  While great events go grandly by;
  These tiny meteors streak the sky,
While giant suns unnoticed roll.

How often little passions flare
  Across our firmament and cease;
  While love's still lamps of light and peace,
In storm and cairn, hang ever there.

XXVIII.
IN DAYS OF OLD.

Are those old days for ever gone
  When Venus moved amid her doves,
  And, playing there, the soft-limbed loves
Made beautiful the summer lawn;

When all the earth was bright with flowers;
  And all the heaven with blue and flame;
  And on the air rich perfumes came ;
And sweet birds built in quiet bowers;

And every tree was filled with song;
  And every brook was jubilant,
  And poured its silver-noted chant
Where'er its waters moved along;

And insects hummed; lithe lizards slid
  Through grass and stones in green and gold
  Of living colours ; nothing old
Could sense of ageless youth forbid;

And all things brought their treasures there,
  Of matchless beauty, priceless worth ;
  And at her feet they poured them forth—
Their goddess and their minister?

So in the past : and now it seems,
  The while we picture this as so,
  We deem that old-world gold and glow
Has passed for ever like our dreams.

Is it not rather sight is dim
  And rests upon the sombre veil?—
  He saw, the ancient, and we fail
To see the beauty, clear to him.

I know that still Love's girdle binds
  True hearts to true, and sweet souls yet
  Will make us all life's ills forget,
And lift the gloom from shadowed minds :

And still in many a homely home,
  'Mid birds and flowers, our Venus moves;
  And round about her knees the loves
Play, heedless of the years to come.

XXIX.
LOVE TRIUMPHANT.

"" 'Mid birds and flowers' and only there?"
  You ask me. No, I make reply,
  Love's kingdom knows no boundary,
And queens of love are everywhere.

In city's heart, on barren plain,
  On snowy waste, in golden vale,
  Alike is told the ancient tale
In varied version; Love must reign.

In crowded dens, where fever creeps,
  From bed to bed, with fiery breath
  That cools before the face of Death,
Where joyless childhood starves and weeps,

Or worse, weeps *not* where long abuse
  Of God's good gifts has dried all tears
  With fire, not love, and tender years
Seem old in that dread round of use :

Here tenderly some woman moves,
  Awaking wonder, or some mood
  Of dull compliance—gratitude
She asks not from her loveless loves.

Think not to her the flowers' sweet breath
  Is nothing, still in Memory's glades
  Their perfume floats nor beauty fades,
Recalled within the dens of death.

To her they come as messages
  From distant lands—how far, how near—
  And, knowing all, her way is clear
To choose a path in fields like these :

To other eyes with evil stored,
  To her a garden, needing care,
  That she may tend and gather there
A posy for her waiting Lord.

On arid sand and trackless snow
  Love universal holds her sway,
  As in the past, and souls obey,
And to a purer influence bow.

XXX.
LOVE AND HOPE.

Pandora, what a dower of ill
  Was thine upon thy marriage day—
  That box where all life's evils lay
Abiding time to work their will.

Life marred for ever by thy good;
  All curses loosed when thou wert blest—
  First mortal, dooming all the rest
To Dead Sea apples for their food

Yes, even so; but yet remained
  Two blessed compensations; one—
  Love—thine already, here begun,
And, with all evil, Hope was gained.

XXXI.
LOVE THE RESTORER.

Œnone and Penelope,
  True souls whose faith the bards rehearse
  On monuments of deathless verse,
How dear are your sweet names to me.

O faithful souls; O loving hearts;
  Your trust so long, so sorely tried
  At length was surely satisfied—
Your loves have found their counterparts?

How can it be? shall false be true,
  Can broken faith be whole again?
  Shall aching hearts be freed from pain?
Can old loves e'er give place to new?

Can that which has been be undone?
  Can words once spoken be unsaid?
  Can life proceed where life is dead,
Or heat flow from a burnt-out sun?

Can boundless time release the years
  That grief has stored, or festal songs
  Be free from that old wail of wrongs,
Or smiles destroy all trace of tears?

It seems not: how things transient seem
  As lasting; in another sphere
  Will evil, felt as deathless here,
Fall off and show us but a dream?

I know not, guess not, but I know
  There is some mighty power in love
  To cleanse and heal, and souls may move,
And, through progressive cycles, grow.

XXXII.
RIZPAH.

Mother, whose love no danger knows,
  No horror shrinks from, watching there,
  As others watch a treasure rare,
The treasure of thy perished sons.

From barley-harvest till the rain,
  For them, for thee, sheds pitying tears,
  The vulture hovers, swoops and nears,
And prowls the lean jackal, in vain.

Thy loving memory will reclothe
  Those wasting forms in noble dress
  Of royal princely manliness,
Nor draw from that which others loathe.

Still thine ; by thine own bosom fed ;
  From thee their strength ; O mother good !
And Earth contests thy motherhood,
And robs thee of thy cherished dead.

Can naught avail to bring relief?
  Thy heart, that only will not break:
  Thy awful vigil for their sake:
Thy tearless eyes wiped dry by grief!

Can nothing help thy stricken ones;
  No prayer unframed, no gift at all,
  The past with all its ill recall,
And give thee once again thy sons?

Thy mother's love for them would drain
  The cup of death, and more than death,
  To bring again the parted breath,
And flush with life those veins again.

XXXIII.
TIME'S CURSE AND BLESSING.

This is Time's curse, to weigh us down,
  With eyes averted from the sky
  That stretches still its blue on high
Above us, though we smile or frown :

This is Time's curse, to take the glow
  From summer lives, and touch our souls
  With that earth-fog, that slowly rolls
Across the fairest scene we know :

This is Time's curse, to know the best
  Is fading surely while, unmoved,
  We suffer all the things we loved
To pass, nor follow in their quest :

This is Time's curse, to over-pass
  Life's freshness; lose the heights of love ;
  To cling below and fail above,
And make a bed of withered grass :

Now Time is victor, senses fail
  To answer impotent desires,
  With no delight in fading fires
That pale as all things mortal pale.

This is Time's curse, but, yet behind,
  I know a blessing somewhere waits;
  Our feet are nearing still the gates
To which our aching eyes are blind.

This is Time's blessing, past all worth,
  To bring again the love we gave;
  An arm to lead us to the grave
As gently as we led it forth :

This is Time's blessing, growing near,
  That all we counted once as ours,
  Unseen, has gained eternal powers
Of life and love more truly dear :

This is Time's blessing, just to feel,
  When all is failing, that the true
  Awaits us; old things all made new;
Old visions permanent and real.

Love seen a moment, here its power
  Is never gauged nor fully shown;
  But there we know it as our own,
In its unfading wealth of flower.

XXXIV.
PAIN.

What is this mystery of pain?
  For blessing or for punishment?
  What mission has it; what intent;
And can it ever be in vain?

Is it some discipline for good;
  Or only here to work us ill?
  Has it a purpose to fulfil,
Forerunning some beatitude ?

Is it a blessing in disguise ;
  A friend in some unfriendly form ?
  Is there a lull within the storm
To those that cross its boundaries?

Is it a penalty we pay;
  Or just a sign of special care,
  Some pruning for the garden *there*,
Some cutting of the waste away?

Is it a mark of ancient war,
  Of ceaseless feud, that ever so
  Pursues its fight, with blow on blow,
To bring us down from what we are ?

Or, is it not a constant sign
  That we are more than that we see,
  And that immortal self must be
Encompassed with a mortal shrine?

Does outraged law its power assert,
  Avenge its violation thus;
  Or, does the message come to us
With blessing laden, not with hurt?

Is it a touch of quickened life,
  The beating of our prisoned soul,
  That will not bear to feel control—
A ceaseless flesh-and-spirit strife ?

Is it our share in Nature's groan
  And travail till the night be past,
  And that great morning break at last,
And God and Nature be at one?

Is it—O can it be a rod
  Of anger? or a healing touch
  Of that Physician? Shrinking much,
We call it still the Hand of God.

That awful baptism of pain,
  And cup of suffering, like His own,
  Christ gave to those who asked a throne—
Not surely cruel gift nor vain;

And unto one the crown was given
  Of martyrdom, and one was blest
  With that great vision of the rest,
Unresting, of the saints in heaven.

Ah! surely He hath borne our griefs,
  Our sorrows carried, He has known
  And made our pains His very own,
And from His treasury dealt reliefs.

O mystery of doubt and pain,
  Whence is it? wherefore? who may say
  Till God shall roll the clouds away,
And all the hidden things be plain?

O mystery of pain and doubt,
  How can we ever solve it here?
  How hope to feel our powers clear
To work the mighty problem out?

How can we dream the why to prove?
  At most we guess it, yet we know,
  Beyond all fears, it must be so,
That somewhere moves a Hand of Love.

XXXV.
WRESTLING.

The light is coming ! Light will come
  And meet us while we toil and shrink,
  Yet strive to reach it—through some chink
The light must touch us from our home.

How long the way is ! longer too
  By our own making, wandering wide,
  And helplessly, where paths divide ;
No glimmer yet to help us through.

And sometimes, 'twixt the dark and light,
  We meet the Man and wrestle there,
  Convulsed in agony of prayer,
Unuttered from its very might.

"Thou shalt not leave me ! let the gleam
  Of daylight widen. Let the flood
  Of fuller morning strike my blood
With life, from its all-living stream—

"Not leave me till thou bless me!" This,
  I think, is even why He waits,
  For violence to storm the gates
Of entrance to the courts of bliss.

Henceforth, perchance, to bear the mark
  Of pain endured, the sign He gave
  And set upon His victor-slave,
Who strove for service through the dark ;

Who, striving, won when Nature failed :
  Who knew the Man with whom he strove
  For blessing, Type and Source of love;
Who saw God's face and yet prevailed.

XXXVI.
RAPTURE.

I sometimes think that they who miss
  The depth of suffering, often lose
  The height of rapture, scaled by those
Whose feet have known the dread abyss.

"Out of the deep" the voice has gone
  In darkness to the nameless Name;
  And from the summit's brow of flame
The victor-cry is carried on.

A glimpse of glory in the night,
  Just seen an instant, veiled again;
  A thrill of joy across the pain;
A throbbing of some inward light;

A thunder-cloud, whose heart of fire
  Reveals itself in sudden rifts ;
  A vapour that a moment lifts,
And shows the end of all desire :

So in the darkness. What in light,
  When wrestling ceases, gaining there
  The more than answer to a prayer
Poured forth in agony and night?

Prayer wholly voiceless now, no boon
  To pray for, nothing unfulfilled
  Remaining, when the soul was thrilled
With that full blaze of cloudless noon.

Prayer hushed in worship, lost in bliss,
  And self forgotten in the gleam
  Of that eternal glory-stream
That flows from that high world to this.

So, sometimes to the stricken soul
  God's compensations come and show
  A something others may not know,
An earnest of a nearing goal.

O mystery of love and pain !
  How can we think or sing aright,
  Where light is darkness, darkness light,
As God to us is hid or plain?

XXXVII.
EARTH'S TREASURE.

Thou holdest in thy rugged crust,
  Dark Earth, our dearest and our best ;
  In thy true bosom there is rest,
And dust can mix with kindred dust.

O Earth, Earth, Earth, we hold thee dear
  For that thou keepest, where thy flowers
  Bloom from the dust we counted ours,
Whose feet with ours have wandered here.

No more, no more ; ah ! now beneath
  Thou foldest them in awful rest;
  Thou dost not mock them; 'tis thy best
Thou givest, in this living wreath.

O Earth, Earth, Earth, we envy thee ;
  We can but bring the gift of tears,
  But thine, of flowers, the generous years
Endue with grace increasingly.

XXXVIII.
HEART MUSIC.

Sing, heart, the birds are singing, sing,
  For life is young and time is long,
  Nay, endless both, and blessed song
Is the expression of the spring.

Sing, heart, the world is singing, lo !
  The great song-angel passed along,
  And woke the silent lips to song,
And thou, my heart, art dumb with woe.

Sing, heart, the earth renews her years;
  Though yonder mounds our dear ones hide,
  She stars them with her "daisies pied,"
And says, "Forget not, yet your tears

"May catch the light, that not for you,
  Nor less for them, has ceased to be,
  Whose fulness steeps the crystal sea,
Nor lights alone but passes through."

Sing, heart, your oneness thus is shown
  In truer harmony with these,
  Who rest beyond Time's broken seas,
Beyond the dark and dread unknown.

Sing, heart, all nature sings ; the birds
  And insects lead thee ; all the air
  In sweet vibration trembles there,
With that great song whose notes are words :

Words like that wondrous spirit-speech,
  One voice, that, unto each who heard,
  Unloosed the clearest, sweetest word;
The needed message unto each.

Glad Nature touch our tongues with flame,
  Nor let us shameful silence keep;
  But add our tribute to the deep,
To swell the song we cannot name.

Sing, heart, it may be thou hast lain
  Too long in thankless sorrow ; sing,
  And pour in sound the hidden thing
That wakes thee to thyself again.

XXXIX.
SWALLOWS.

Sweet spring returns to us once more,
  And on her winds the swallows come,
  To greet us in our northern home,
And gain a welcome as of yore.

Dear birds, so fresh from southern skies,
  How cold must seem these clouds of ours;
  How bare our land, whose timorous flowers
Still fear to look with open eyes.

Yet, hearts are warm and fires aglow,
  And shelter sure; and we would fain
  Believe the summer here again,
Before we well have lost the snow.

Sweep from the vault above us, spread,
  And dip your wings in yonder stream,
  And flash the light, with sudden gleam,
From breast and wing, and burnished head :

Skim past the shadows of the woods,
  Rise into light again, nor fear
  To cherish household loves, and rear
About our homes your helpless broods.

Why leave us when the leaves are sere?
  Why leave us with the shortening days?
  All pass, but living memory stays,
And through all seasons love is here.

XL.
NATURE'S MOODS.

Is not the wild storm's spirit one
  With that which broods above the calm :
  The loud-voiced thunder's awful psalm
A sweet bird's song in deeper tone?

I know not, yet sometimes to me
  These moods seem Nature's changeful dress,
  In which she clothes her loveliness—
One beauty shown us variously.

The many sounds, the shifting keys,
  In which her mind itself reveals; —
  Now in the rolling thunder peals,
Now in the still small voice of peace—

All seem from one deep source to spring;
  One living fount, where all are hid,
  To issue as occasion bid,
For fitting time, the fitting thing.

And so her garb, now robe of light,
  Now deepest purple, wrapping there
  That form we know is always fair,
That wears its beauty day and night.

Her voice is always that of love,
  In many tones, whose music stirs,
  And brings about those feet of hers,
All who within her influence move.

XLI.
LOVE'S WEALTH.

Flowers of the spring, whose tender hues
  First touch the scale of colour low,
  Scarce warmer than the melting snow,
To deepen into reds and blues.

As skies grow brighter, summer suns
  Pour gold along the panting plains,
  And warmth and vigour stir the veins
Through which the glow of gladness runs.

Gold in exchange for gold, and blue
  To match the azure overhead,
  And red, as sunset's brightest red,
And royal purple, hue for hue.

Love answers love, love love begets,
  Love's gold is never cast away,
  Though hidden many a weary day,
'Tis found, perchance, when daylight sets.

Love love begets, her talents she
  In patience trusts, her gold she gives
  Ungrudgingly, her gold that lives
And gathers sweetest usury.

XLII.
LOVE'S SUPREMACY.

All things rejoice in beauty—sound,
  Or form, or colour, all express
  A truth, in outward loveliness,
And girt with all adornment round :

Such beauty as one sees in spring,
  When Hope and Faith together meet,
  And bring their treasures to our feet,
And woods with love-songs throb and ring :

When every bird and every tree
  With love pulsates, and quickened lives
  Proclaim their joy, and Nature strives
To lift the gloom and struggle free.

When human hearts with wilder glee,
  And deeper longings, know the truth
  That, self-proclaimed in days of youth,
Asserts Love's true supremacy.

O budding world, O living love,
  O loving life that, waking so,
  Makes all things spring, rejoice, and grow,
And to their full fruition move!

XLIII.
THE NIGHTINGALE.

O bird that, when the primrose pale
  Gems bank and copse, from o'er the sea
  Bringest thy gift of melody
To greet the spring, O nightingale!

Thy voice at times is touched with woe;
  At times with joy; a tender tale
  Thou tellest, O sweet nightingale!
I listen, and I cannot go.

And now thy note is one of wail;
  What meaneth this? Make answer, why
  Is joy so near to agony?
Thou knowest both, true nightingale.

What is this mystery of thine?
  O tell me, ere the stars grow pale,
  For it may be, O nightingale,
Thy secret is akin to mine.

And thou canst sing; while I must fail
  To utter what my heart contains;
  But thy full burden, joys and pains,
Thou pourest forth, blest nightingale!

Yet memory will at times rehearse
  The past too truly, sweet notes quail
  Before thy passion, nightingale,
Thy song is then a broken verse.

O mighty love! O heart so frail
  That breakest with its ecstasy !—
  I think that thou hast sung to me
Some of thy secret, nightingale.

XLIV.
THE BUTTERFLY.

The butterfly that bursts its shell
  And rises, from a mimic death,
  To float, upon the perfumed breath
Of June, above some flowery dell,

Must feel within itself some change;
  Some unfamiliar sense of power,
  Inherited in that wild hour
That gave it unrestricted range :

So, when the husk of self is riven,
  We rise on Love's unfolded wings,
  And see the upturned gaze of things,
And float between the earth and heaven.

XLV.
LOVE'S PATIENCE.

Love is impatient! Nay, the years
  She counts as days, and so forecasts
  The future, while probation lasts,
That she can find no place for tears :

She knows the power of look and word
  To bridge the hours, like sweetest chime
  That marks the flying course of time
With music looked for, loved when heard,

And loved when, dying far away,
  Its echoes linger, float, and fall,
  And rise, in harmony with all
That links to-morrow with to-day.

O time of waiting, not uncheered,
  For tokens sweet, from lips and eyes,
  Seem openings to that Paradise
To which our feet have daily neared.

XLVI.
THE GLOW-WORM.

There, where the bracken slowly turns
  From green to gold, 'neath summer skies
  (The gold of all, that few men prize),
The glow-worm's steadfast lantern burns

I saw it in the early spring;
  Now, in the glory of the year;
  In autumn, too, its light was here;
And count it nigh a constant thing.

It always speaks to me of home
  And welcome ; Hope and Memory meet
  About its glow, and all things sweet
Spring from its light, that beacons "Come."

I know a light in heart and room
  So like to this, but truer still;
  It fails not when the nights are chill,
But brighter burns in winter's gloom.

XLVII.
LOVE'S TREASURE.

"Say what is thy belovèd more
  Than all belovèds ? wherefore prate
  Of thy love's music? is it great
And others of a feebler score ?

"All love is love, and mine from thine
  May differ but in such degree
  As scarce disturbs equality,
Or even show the balance mine.

"What more is thy belovèd, say,
  Than all belovèds? Wherefore sing
  As though thy treasure made the spring,
Its absence brought the winter day?"

Nay, nothing more, but more to me
  Than all belovèds; I rejoice
  In that I know another's voice
May praise another equally.

XLVIII.
LOVE'S ESTIMATE.

I know not, and can never know,
  Which love is greater, thine or mine—
  True soul that, through the storm and shine,
Hath held to me, in joy, in woe.

I may not say another's love
  Is not as great as thine for me,
  Or less than is my love for thee,
Yet scarcely can it greater prove.

It may be that all loves possess
  Peculiar treasure, and alone
  Some special gift may call their own,
In all its power to soothe or bless :

It may be that the good or grace
  We prize so much, so proudly wear,
  Is not the gem that others bear,
As fitly, in its honoured place.

Thy tender knowledge of the best;
  Thy finer tact and woman's skill;
  Achieve, without the show of will,
And fill me with a sense of rest

From long experience surely drawn,
  That when the darkness gathers most
  Thy love is brightest—at what cost
I know not, till the nearing dawn

Shall thy self-sacrifice reveal,
  And show aright thy woman's gift,
  To find within the cloud the rift,
The music in the thunder-peal.

XLIX.
LOVE'S HARMONY.

O mother praying for thy son !
  O son that criest to be free !
  We bring our troubles, Lord, to Thee,
And Thou canst make the answer one.

For things divine we yearn and call;
  Thou knowest all our needs, our cares,
  And Thou canst take conflicting prayers
And bring a harmony from all.

O mighty, perfect Sacrifice !
  O Love that, with Thy latest breath,
  Didst wrest the victory from Death
And give us life, Thine own life's price!

Thou givest life; Thou givest love;
  Eternal both, from Thee they spring,
  And unto Thee their treasures bring;
The Source, the End, to which we move.

L.
THE SHAPING OF LIFE.

O can it be love's crown to grieve
  For what was once but now is lost;
  To know our treasure by the cost
Of suffering, when our dear ones leave?

And must it always come to this,
  To lose or leave our dearest things ;
  To take, or see them take, the wings;
Ourselves to go or these to miss ?

Can dower of love or doom of pain,
  Or any lot that falls to man,
  Be aught but part of some vast plan
That compasses his greatest gain?

Is pain for pain's sake : love for love's :
  Or are they, could we understand,
  Tools in the Master Workman's Hand,
To fit us to our proper grooves?

Perhaps to those All-Seeing Eyes
  Some pattern of our life exists ;
  Some clear portrayal, past the mists,
Of that to which our souls may rise.

LI.
DOUBT AND HOPE.

So have I chanted, all too long,
  Love's praise, and multiplied in vain
  Words fruitless. Life is full of pain,
And death is near and hatred strong.

Can love bring back the days bygone?
  Can love do more than lightly heal
  The wounds of love, that know the steel,
Albeit the sword is long withdrawn?

Can love upgather water spent?
  Can love do more, at best, than hide
  Her grief, by spreading garments wide,
Or give for peace a half-content?

Can sullied snow again be fair?
  Can touch of love the bloom replace
  That lay, God's gift, on that sweet face—
His fruit—how good He saw it there?

Can love the fallen life restore?
  Can love atone for past offence,
  Or bring again the innocence
That robed us in the days of yore?

Can any love the past undo ?
  Can any love the future bring
  With that old freshness, when the spring
Of life was making all things new?

Can love the locust-eaten years
  Wrest from our store of all things ill?
  Can love again the channels fill,
Worn by the flow of frequent tears?

We cannot tell, but long and pray
  (And hope would weaker doubt disprove)
  The purifying flame of love
May wholly burn life's dross away.

LII.
LOVE'S STREAM.

My love is just a little stream,
  That threads its way 'twixt stone and stone
  At times with song, but oft with moan,
And touched with shadow and with gleam.

Now hollowed to a glassy bath,
  That holds the sweet moon's placid face,
  And now concealed, but for the trace
Of greener herbage round its path.

Now shadowed by a scar on high,
  That frowns above it, with the gloom
  Of some old, strange, forbidding tomb,
Whose emblems speak mortality:

But, just beyond the tomb's black gates,
  It opens into light so full,
  Such rippling sparkle; who so dull,
But feels the life that palpitates?

And widens into broad expanse;
  And bears its flowers upon its breast;
  But ever longing still for rest,
Unsatisfied with gleam and glance:

And rolls with gathering purpose on,
  Between the banks that curb its flow,
  And give it depth, and keep it so,
With steadfast faith, unswerving will,

And through it all a deepening key
  Of music other voices stills ;
  A growing murmur past the hills;
A message from the nearing sea.

LIII.
THE SELFLESSNESS OF LOVE,

So have I dreamed Love's waking dream,
  And still her spell is round me cast ;
  Though all things perish, Love shall last,
And *be*, when these no longer *seem*.

Love is not joy alone, nor pain;
  Love may possess and Love may lose ;
  Love must accept and cannot choose
Between a seeming loss or gain.

Is Love to self a minister?
  Looks she not on another's things ?
  And all her dearest treasures brings
Her gold, her frankincense, her myrrh ?

Self-sacrifice ! ah, this is love ;
  To wish ourselves accursed, if so
  We might but lessen others' woe,
And lift the cross they cannot move.

Who seeks his life shall lose it. He
  Who seeks not love, shall find again
  The seed he cast, not lost, nor vain,
But multiplied mysteriously:

Shall surely see with open eyes
  (No longer blinded with his tears)
  His love with all the growth of years,
And glorified, about him lies.

TO LOVE'S SOURCE. (I JOHN IV. 7.)

O Last, O First, to Thee we bow,
  From Thee proceed and to Thee tend
  All loves, of love the Source, the End,
The Alpha, the Omega Thou !

Thou sendest forth Thy gifts that move
  In orbits that return on Thee,
  That seek again the primal Sea,
The fathomless Abyss of Love.

Love's Source, love's End, Thou then must be
  Love perfect, All-Divine, complete;
  In Thee all wealth of love must meet,
And all our best be part of Thee.

Love All-Diffusive, touching all;
  O blessed hearts, so pure and clear,
  That keep the mirrored Image here
In beauty, till the shadows fall.

All love, we know, in its degree,
  Has caught some faint reflex of rays,
  Some brightness from the jewel's blaze,
Whose heart of light is hid with Thee.

This yearning, when with passion thrilled ;
  This lacking note in love's high chant;
  This something more; this nameless want ;
Can only be by Thee fulfilled.

We rise from what is less to more,
  And grasping, with a true intent,
  Thy line of love, by sure ascent
Our feet may touch the blessed shore.

Not strange to Thee, our grief, Who kept
  Lone vigil on the mountain there;
  Not strange our agony of prayer,
Our stricken love, for Thou hast wept.

O Love, Thou stoppedst at the bier,
  And turned a victory, seeming won;
  And to the mother gave the son,
And so asserted mastery here.

One came of old with orbless eyes,
  And laid a hand upon our own,
  And led us to a feared unknown;
But Thou hast claimed again the prize :

And Death, but as Thy herald now,
  Proclaims to every honoured guest
  The marriage-feast and Thy behest,
And lays the faded garments low.

Ah, Lord, what heritage is ours !
  We move engirt with mystery,
  But could we see as spirits see,
If our poor eyes had subtler powers,

How should we know, when sorrows fall,
  When losses crush us, when we cry,
  Like helpless children asking "why?"
That yet Thy love is over all :

That what we least can understand,
  The darkness sometimes o'er us laid
  In silence, is the cooling shade,
And presence of Thy nearer hand!

We love, we lose; the light we see
  Thou showest, soon perchance withdrawn;
  With face upturned we wait the dawn
That shows all light, all love, with Thee.

SHORTER POEMS

A CHARACTER SKETCH

SHE loved to gaze upon the stars,
  That brighter grew with deep'ning night ;
  And sorrowed when the early light
Of morning spread in golden bars.

She cared not for the glaring day ;
  But loved the mystery of the dark,
  That faded when the soaring lark
Cleft with swift wing the melting grey.

With sweetest music ever thrilled
  The blackness ; every mystic sound
  In her an eager listener found,
With weird enjoyment wholly filled.

Nor looked she on the foam-flecked flood,
  That tumbled down the broken steep,
  But bent above the awful deep,
Within the shadow of the wood,

Whose wave some guilty secret holds,
  And whispers hoarsely all the day,
  And sobs the hours of dark away,
And wraps its prey in blackened folds.

MARGARET

HAST thou forgotten, then, that one bright night
Long years ago,
When in these arms I held my one delight
(Ah! since my woe)?
Hast thou forgotten, then the moon was low,
  And touched with light my darling's trembling lips,
But I was held in shadow, that I know,
  In token of that drawing near eclipse?

Thou hast forgotten, yes, the past is past,
O Margaret!
With me alone remembrance still must last,
Thou canst forget:
But all the past is present with me yet,
  And memory, seeking like tide-conquered river
Her backward path, reveals my Margaret
  Before a broken troth was hers for ever.

At times I ask, is this the Margaret
Of days gone by;
The light on which my eager gaze was set
In darkest sky?
She hath her beauty, as of old, but I
  Know she is changed in the angel's ken,
And I would search through all eternity
  To find my Margaret as I knew her then.

Had I been false to thee, as thou hast been,
Not with sweet smile,
And hand outstretched to greet thee, had I seen
Thee suffer while:
Had I been false to thee my coward guile
  Had smitten me with shame upon the face,
And I had paused to hear .thy voice the while
  I bowed my head in merited disgrace.

Farewell, O Margaret of the changing faith;
'Tis well for thee
Thy first love perished by an icy breath
While thou wert free
(Or deemdst thyself so); may thy latest be
  More lasting; for to thee the hour has come
When changing love were changeless misery,
  To thee a stranger in a homeless home.

AMY

THE ever-floating glory of her hair—
  Now streaming out upon the summer wind,
Now hiding half the sweet face nestling there—
    And that quick twinkle of her clear blue eye,
    Behind the shining golden tracery
  That falls adown her neck and is entwined
With wild-flower gems, most delicate of hue,
Wind-flowers, forget-me-nots, and violets blue,
  And (peeping out half-hidden by the fold
That binds it willing prisoner) hawthorn bloom,
  Whose tender petals mingle with the gold,
And breathe a blessing in a rich perfume;
  The rosy lips, and that provoking pout,
Do deck a beauty of so bright a mould,
  We gaze unconsciously in quaintest doubt
If such a fairy-form be human-souled.

IDA

IMPERIAL Ida ! not by constant flash
  Of liquid beauty doth thine eye command,
But gazing ever from beneath a lash,
  Silken and sable, with a steadfast glow
    (Not proud, but passionless, serenely pure),
  All men before thy perfect beauty bow.
    In native majesty thou art secure,
  Thou bear'st no golden sceptre in thy hand,
  And wear'st no diadem about thy brow,
And yet thy queen-like grace hath greater power
  Than sword-supported royal mandates have;
  And those long tresses o'er thy forehead wreathe
    A nobler crown than gem-enriched gold
(A glorious night where just one stainless flower
    Shines out, in never-lessening beauty, cold).
Thou need'st no precious ore, nor priceless stone,
Thine is a beauty beautiful alone.

PASSING

THE days go ever on and on,
And swiftly pass—
The sands of life that early run
Through Time's turned glass :

And these that yet remain are just
The grains that stay
A moment, ere they join the dust
That rolls away.

SUNLESS

GREY dawn before the horse's fervent feet
Beat flakes of fire from out the cloud-paved road.
   Grey dusk that follows in the flaming track
Of flying wheels that spurn the western marge.
   Grey dawn, cold, pure, severe and passionless.
   Grey dusk, of heat and fury emptied, void
Of hope and yearning pleasures, satiate
With love and hate and all things.
Dusk and dawn
The end and the beginning of a day ;
The end and the beginning of a life
How often, and between the fire and smoke,
The steadfast glory and the sputtering torch.

   Dawn, ere the bright twin children, Light and Hope,
The offspring of the Morn, are born to Earth.
   Dusk, when the echoes of her hollow courts
Are waked no more with laughter ; Hope is dead,
And Light departed in the flaming car.

   Grey dawn; grey dusk; then things seem what they are,
With native beauty robed or horror wreathed;
No added loveliness nor heightened wrath,
No sunny ripples and no folds of gloom,
Tamper with naked truth, but all things stand
Cold as a grey rock in a land of ice.

Dawn; splinter'd sticks in order, jetty coal
To crown them, waiting for the torch of day.
  Dusk; ashen embers, black and charred remains,
Impoverished of their heat by fiery lips.
  Between; the myriad licking tongues of flame
Unsatisfied, and wreathed braids of smoke
Unsteadfast, false, in miraged loveliness.

  Aspirest thou, O man, for light and heat ?
Art thou an eagle that thou woo'st the sun?
Aspirest thou, O moth, for candle-flame ?
Thy ashes shall no more arise to life,
But thou shalt know scorched wings and blinded eyes
And enter darkness through the gate of light.

  Dawn with the calm, clear brow and dewy smile
Before the battle and the roar of wheels.
  Dusk with the bloody streaks upon her face
And on *her* brow "experience" deeply graved
In dusty channels, and her poor wan lips
Parched with the burning drought,
Grey dawn; grey dusk;
What endless images of life are yours
(That all may see, but none may tell aright) :
Dawn for life's spring-time, dusk for wasted age,
Noon for the heat of manhood, and deep night
To spread her black wing o'er a lonely grave
Where beat the echoes of a lonely deep.

IN MEMORIAM. A. M. M.

"And Jesus called a little child unto Him," —ST. MATT. xvi ii. 2.
"The peace of God, which passeth all understanding." —PHIL. iv. 7.

WE thank Thee. May no breath of murmur stir
  The stillness; Father, this is not Thy rod
But Thy most soothing hand; Thou givest her
  That which ourselves desire, "the peace of God."

PENELOPE. (A FRAGMENT.)

THE Summer fades and Winter bares the trees,
And Spring reclothes them, and again the heat
And glory of the Summer come and pass,
And Autumn follows with her yellow robes,
But he comes not to me.
Slow wane the hours ;
Slow the sad days and weary years go by;
And yet not slowly Care's unfaltering hand
Draws furrows on this brow.
Why comes he not?
He liveth yet ; not in Troy's dreary siege,
Not by th' assassin's hand has he gone forth
To wander through the darkness and the mist.
  I know he lives. I feel his life in mine.
The warmth of his great heart still strengthens me,
And I live on.
My lord, Ulysses, come!
Delay not longer, thy Penelope
Is sore beset and waits thy forceful hand
And never-failing sword to rout these men
These coward men—that hem me round and say,
"He cannot live," again, "and, if he live,
Why comes he not?" and then, with faithless eyes
Full of hypocrisy and cowardice,
"Not so would I;" they say, "not thus alone
The time should pass unheeded," ay, and more,
They vex me with their importunities.

* * * * *

But when thou comest all this leaden time,
This hateful present, will be turned to past
And flooded over with the tide of love.

TIME—A RIVER

TIME, methinks, is just a river
Where the bubbles burst and shiver,
While the great thoughts live for ever
   Floating on the changing face ;
Down the flowing stream they fly,
Battling with adversity,
Or unmoved go grandly by,
   Calm, and victors in the race.

They, the poets of the past,
Spake, and lo ! their words will last,
In the tranquil hollow glassed,
   Or upon the circling foam
Riding, where some inward life
Beats the waters into strife;
Where the depths with passion rife
   Speak a troubled spirit's home.

All our thoughts and actions flow;
Trembling down the stream they go ;
Sink beneath or ever show
   Sparkling on the crest of Time;
And, at times we backward gaze
Where, upon the river's face,
All the waters seem ablaze
   With a memory sublime.

Shadowed underneath the wood,
Lying in the darksome flood,
Like a spectre stained with blood,
   Hides some evil passion past :
Here where lulls the babbling stream,
Silvered with the falling beam,
Dwells the reflex of a dream
   Seen in youth that faded fast.

Here, methinks, the angers roll;
Here the throbbings of the soul
Shake the surface, and the whole
   Moveth like a living thing:
Joy and Sorrow, Hate and Love,
In the heaving bosom move,
And the waves are gold above
   With the ceaseless glistening.

When we drift adown the tide,
Running far and stretching wide,
While the changing waters glide
   Over ashes. dim and cold;
Is the past a track of light,
Or a shadow of the night,
Or a spot of holy light,
   Like an angel garment's fold?

RETROSPECT

LIFE seems at times one vast regret
For something, unaccomplished yet,
We should have done, and so we fret
Our lives away :
Or something we have rashly done,
That better had been left alone—
Been vexed, perhaps, with a loving one—
Some distant day.

Some god-like purpose broken through ;
Some yielding, when Temptation threw
Her nets about us ; something new
That slew the old ;
The old, forsaken, lying dead,
And yet not wholly vanquishèd,
That met us ever as we fled,
A spectre cold.

Some doubt of faith ; some broken trust;
Some bitter word, we knew unjust,
To one who lieth low in dust—
So silent now :
The faith was proved, alas ! too well ;
The broken trust is broken still ;
And who shall now our sorrow tell
To one laid low ?

One vast regret ; one sorrow rife ;
One lifelong agony and strife ;
One yearning for the fuller life,
That comes so slow :
And then the hope to right the wrong ;
To heal the discord of the song;
To feel, by full forgiveness, strong
Before we go.

A MEMORY

FLOWER o' the valley that seest the lightning leap from the rocks;
Flower o' the valley that hearest the crackling of thunder shocks;
Flower o' the valley that bendest thy head to the rush of rains,
Breathest thy scent to the mountains, pourest thy tears to the plains.

Flower o' the valley that feelest the mist-woven clouds of the height
Trail in their grandeur across thee, leaving thee holy and white—
Thou, at the foot of the mountain, hearest, as if from the dead,
Voices of mystical import that reach thee from overhead.

Thou, O sweet flower o' the valley, minglest not in the wrath,
Scapest, yet seest, the flame of the white-furrowed lightning path;
Thee would I take to myself from the fury of torrent and sun;
Flower o' the valley I pluck thee, for thou dost remind me of *one*.

> "For with Thee is the well of life, and in Thy light shall we see light." - PSALM xxxvi. 9.

LIFE from the Well of Life, more perfect light
In Thy Light, give us these, good Lord, we pray.

Life to the full, the ever-beating heart
Of boundless sympathy and throbbing heat
And unaccomplished, unassuaged desire ;
Undying life, that never groweth sere
Nor withereth till it bloom in fulness.
Light
In Thy Light, to discriminate the truth
From error, nor count wholly base nor black
The soiled whiteness of a lower world,
Or darkness flecked with heaven-rays.
Light to see,
And life to act and work beneath the light.
Thou hast the Well of Life; Thou boldest all
The countless motions of the universe
Within Thy Fount. And Thou renewest life,
As Thou renewest light from day to day
To flood Thy waiting world.
Great Source of all,

First Cause, Sustainer through all timeless time,
Fathomless Well of Life and Fount of Light,
In one full stream Thou pourest forth Thyself.

We pray Thee give us thirst to deeply drink.

DROWNED

AGHAST!
    At *something* there in a pool—
A woman, finding rest at last,
    'Mid pond-weeds green and cool :
And my head is sick, and my heart beats fast,
    And the people think me a fool.

A face!
    A face and a tangle of hair
In the wet weeds' cold embrace;
    A stony, yearning, helpless stare,
A craving look for God's good grace,
    On the dead face lying there.

Her name?
    A woman, why ask ye more?
Would ye tell the world the shame
    Of her who this daughter bore?
Let her name perish (as hath her fame)
    In the waters that close her o'er.

[Editor's note: Believed to refer to the drowning of his daughter Carrie Towndrow in 1914.]

TO A.R.W.

THE gift of sight
God grant thee, so, across the years,
Through mist of doubt and rain of tears,
Shalt thou see light:

Life's fullest dower
Be thine, till every mortal sense
Shows poor beside thy affluence
Of spirit power :

And such degree
Of love be reached, that thou canst trace
God's beauty veiled in every face
That fronteth thee.

August 14, 1888.

THE SEARCH

THOUGH doubt for not a moment rests,
  And creeds in loveless strife are clanging,
And dead hopes show like empty nests
  In Winter's naked hedges hanging; —
Still, through the gloom that circles me,
My soul goes forth to find out Thee.

Thou walkest, as of old, the sea,
  And still art on the mountain lonely;
All perfect beauty is of Thee,
  As Thou the Lord of Truth art only:
So, seeking truth in all I see,
I gather it as gift from Thee,

We turn to Thee in bitter pain,
  And when our souls are steeped in shadow,
And when we long for sunlit plain,
  Or cool, and sweetly swarded, meadow:
Thou art as these to those who flee,
In darkness or in drought, to Thee.

And when Death's waves are running high,
  And of Thy might we ask a token,
Ere yet we perish utterly,
  Thy "Peace, be still," again, is spoken :
And lo ! "a great calm" smoothes the sea,
In meek obedience to Thee.

O purple orchids of the Spring;
  O Summer's fuller wealth of blossom ;
O Autumn's golden offering;
  O Snowdrops white on Winter's bosom :
Spring, Summer, Autumn, Winter, see
Thy love for us, these gifts from Thee.

O help me, Lord, to find Thee near,
  And, gaining this, to know Thee nearer,
And having found Thee very dear,
  Still give Thy help to feel Thee dearer;
Till all the mists that circle me,
Are melted at the sight of Thee.

April 11, 1873.

TO—

ALL fair things meet about thee ; O most fair,
  And chief and sweetest, where all loves are sweet
  That lay themselves as offerings at thy feet,
Who dost thy womanhood so lightly wear
In its full wealth of beauty-with an air
  Of native fitness. All the graces meet,
  In rounded loveliness of form, complete
With that expression that thy features bear.
I almost fear to praise thee, for I know
  How well-nigh helpless is all power of speech
To utter deepest thought, and, feeling so,
  That words must ever fail their end to reach,
I fain would be content to sit me low,
  And learn an eloquence thy love can teach.

July 14, 1887.

A SUMMER DAY

Lo! twice to-day God touched His heaven with flame,
  And who regarded? At the early break
  He scattered golden wealth o'er sky and lake
In boundless affluence; when evening came
He traced the mystery of His awful Name
  In fiery characters, and many a flake
  Of crimson, where the pillared poplars shake
Black in the west and so His light proclaim.
So God bestows, and we accept His light,
  And barely marvel—'tis a common thing—
Or, looking lightly, soon forget it quite—
  A sunbeam glancing from a swallow's wing—
Nor heed His Witness, set 'twixt night and night,
  To Love that should not need such witnessing.

THE VISION OF GOD

GOD strews His heaven with stars, His earth with flowers ;
  So, overhead and underneath our feet,
  We see or touch His tokens : O most sweet !
In His true Commonwealth, to know them ours
And all men's—we His children—lo ! He dowers
  Our home with beauty, and about us meet
  His precious things-a gold-paved heavenly street
Each humble pathway, did we use our powers.
Ah me ! the blessing of the pure in heart
  Waits if we would but claim it ! Galahad
    Beheld the Grail and, still, to those who give
Unsullied gaze, the mists roll back and part
  About them, and they see-where all seemed sad—
    The Beatific Vision—God—and live.

March 24, 1887.

Newcastle Chronicle

April 10. 89

A Life, Love, and other Poems. By R. F. T.—This little volume contains several poems of great tenderness and beauty. Amongst the shorter pieces, "Drowned," "A Memory" and "A Character Sketch," are perhaps the finest in the book. (Kegan Paul, Trench, and Co., Paternoster Square, London). Price 3s. 6d.

Scottish Leader

April 13. 89

R. F. T., the author of *A Life, Love, and other Poems* (Kegan Paul, Trench, & Co.) is entitled to the credit of possessing considerable mastery over varied forms of rhythm and metre, but most of his verse is open to the objection which a good many people have felt towards Mr Whistler's "harmonies." It has a good deal of verbal colouring, but fails to lay hold of the reader's sympathies from its lack of definite purpose or design. The best things in the book are the short poems which occupy the last few pages. There is real power as well as charm in the little word-picture entitled "Amy," and the image presented in "Time"—a River, is happily conceived and beautifully wrought out. But we question whether there is any line in this volume which will rescue it from the oblivion that overtakes the greater part of the immense quantity of verse which now annually sees the light.

Manchester Examiner

April 20. 89

A Life, Love, and other poems, by "R. F. T." (London; Kegan Paul, Trench, and Co.). The author apologises for his close imitation of the *In Memoriam*, on the ground of "long and loving familiarity with that noble work." He may be forgiven for his admiration, though the necessity for publishing such palpable reminiscences of the Laureate's style and phrases may not be apparent to the general reader.

Section 2

Reproduction from

'A Garden' and other poems

(Originally published 1892)

A GARDEN

An ancient garden haunts me,
  Where whitest lilies blow;
A little child among them,
  Who walking, wondering so,
Thinks they must be God's angels,
  A-standing row on row.

The pathway, like a ladder,
  Is by the dreamer trod;
Its bars of lily-shadows
  Move as the lilies nod,
And still he walks and wonders
If the ladder leads to God.

The odours make him heavy;
  The little feet move slow;
The butterflies that pass him
  Spill gold-dust as they go—
And, turning to the shadow,
  He leaves behind the glow.

The years have hid the garden,
  Whose lichen-painted door
The child would often enter,
  On sunny days of yore;
In vain, it seems, to find it
  I search for evermore.

At times amid the shadow,
  At times amid the gleam,
Again I see the garden,
  Like some familiar dream,
Where real things seem visions
  And visions real seem.

Sometimes a breath of lilies
  From a basket in the street,
And a weary face about them,
  Will speak of weary feet
That wandered in the garden
  'Mid the odours and the heat.

—

I seek no more the garden;
  Perchance some sweet surprise;
A voice upon the moonlight
  May bid me wake and rise
And follow to the doorway
  Through which the garden lies.

And, as I pass the threshold,
  The well-remembered place
Will lie again before me
  And odours bathe my face,
And dreamy silver moonlight
  Hold night in its embrace.

—

And one within a chamber
  With awe-hushed footsteps trod
And one within a garden
  Beheld the lilies nod
And took the path between them
  To the city of his God.

THE AURORA BOREALIS
(OCTOBER 25, 1870)

[The nights of October 24th and 25th 1870 were remarkable for the great brilliancy and beauty of the aurora borealis, the newspapers of the latter date containing accounts of the phenomenon of the preceding evening: this writer was not fortunate enough to see, but, on the evening of the 25th, he had unusual advantages, during a ten-miles drive, and will never forget the weird grandeur of a belt of fir-trees standing out against a nearly blood-red sky.
The fate of Paris (then in a state of siege) and the recollection of the great battles, only recently fought, associated themselves, he believes, in many minds more or less completely and persistently with the spectacles of those two evenings.]

We left the Ipswich lamps behind, and far away before us
  One after one, the country lights came shyly peeping through
The edge of darkness, and above them, and around and o'er us,
  The orbs of heaven issued from the ever-deep'ning blue.

The skirts of night spread out and touched the far South-East and ended,
  For there a golden glory leaped, with sudden-born desire,
And scaled the vault of Heaven, where the light and shadow blended,
  While eager-eyed we watched it, as the reflex of a fire.

We turned away a moment and behold the day was glowing,
  On our left hand and our right rose a flush of ruddy flame,
Springing upward to an arc, theta was ever deeper growing
  In awfulness and splendour as the flashes went and came.

And it seemed, in the silence of that clear October even,
  The blood that cried for vengeance from the murder-stainèd sod,
God painted, for a protest, on the canvas of His heaven,
  And stars grew wan, beholding there the writing of their God.

An apex of deep blackness into bloody bars diverging,
  A nimbus of red glory playing round a darkened brow;
And from out the flame and darkness two mighty streams emerging,
  Poured forth their crimson torrents on the guilty earth below;

On earth, whose stricken children lay in ebbing life-blood drowning;
  On earth, for aye unmindful of Diviner blood outpoured,
In agony, in scourging, in the piercing and thrown-crowning,
  To seal the awful passion, from the body of her Lord.

'Twas thus I read the writing on the blue walls of God's chamber,
  While His stars grew pale in Heaven with wonder at the sight—
The "Mene, Mene" written where the silent planets clamber:—
  The lurid picture painted to incarnadine the night.

And one found speech and saying, "I should scarce be filled with wonder
  If an angel from the deeps of that circle issued forth,"
My fancy saw the angel, all the blackness torn asunder,
  Stand centred in the ruby beams and gazing on the earth.

And I think though nevermore I may look on that wrath-glory,
  And read the open pages in the record of the sky,
The record of the nations will recount the bloody story
  And the record of my heart will be unclosèd till I die.

AN ARTISTS IDEAL

Harold the artist, Beatrice his bride
(The envy of a little world outside
Their inner world of love and art and rest,
Each satisfied that each possessed the best
Husband or wife), were happy.
Swift the years
Slipped from them; then arose some tender fears
In Harold's conscience, lest his work at last
Would show no excellence quite unsurpassed;
No mighty effort; not one flawless whole,
To prove the artist's hand, but most his soul.
And so his eyes and mind went searching far
To find, 'mid many stars, the brightest star;
'Mid many beauties he with ease might paint
One, full as much a woman as a saint;
One whose unrivalled fairness should embrace
All love with chasteness, majesty with grace.
One day the vision came: a lucky chance
Revealed to him the woman in a glance,
And all his soul with such a sight was filled,
His face reflected what his bosom thrilled.
O'erjoyed, he spake out swiftly : "I have seen
A woman that is surely beauty's queen;
She held her baby; love, if you would sit
Once more as model, I might capture it,
This vision, as I saw it, ere it pass
Like some reflection from a looking-glass.
The face I have quite clearly, you supply

The form, the dress, and each accessory.
I shall then paint a picture that confessed
Will stand alone, my masterpiece, my best."
And so she sat, her child upon her knee,
Day after day, and saw how lost was he
In his ideal; how, as in a dream,
That other face absorbed him in his theme:
Thought herself really jealous, while she knew
Within her heart of hearts, that he was true.
Harold, with artist's eye, failed not to trace
The new expression born into her face,
Undaunted still toiled on; yet, sure of this,
She gave no glance upon that work of his.
At length the task was ended; at his side,
To show her that his true hand had not lied
In execution, he a mirror placed,
And then across the studio he paced
To where the tired wife had her baby laid
Within the cradle's hollow and its shade.
"There, now, my thanks! But you have scarcely yet
Lifted your eyes above the bassinet:
Come, see my perfect woman who has grown
To her completeness; see her, love, and own
My taste is faultless; other's praise be dull
Will seem if you deny her beautiful.
Just for a moment leave your baby there,
And see the face of every face most fair."
She would not leave her baby, 'til twas sweet
To bear him next her heart, to stay its beat:
Thus faced her doom and felt her husband dared,
So wrept was he, to let his soul, unbared,
By this ideal beauty, show to her
He held her only as Art's minister:
His helper, not his equal, then she knew
'Twas his to dream and hers to love and do.

Slowly across the studio she went,
Her lovely face above her baby bent;
From glass to canvas swift her glances sped:
Dress, figure, baby, face and noble head;
Past all dispute, the portrait was the same
On either surface; just a touch of shame
Suffused her face before the sweet surprise,
And love's true lustre lit again her eyes;
"You recognise the portrait, yes, love, you,
The fairest woman that I ever knew,
And"—with a kiss that set her heart at rest—
"In spite of foolish fear, the very best."

A HOLIDAY LYRIC

I.

O these sweet days at the end of July;
Newly-mown meadows;
Fleeting cloud-shadows,
Mocking the chase of eth clouds in the sky;
Here by the stream,
Merrily-musical over the shallows,
Mournfully-musical under the willows
  Bright with its border of "codlins and cream"—
  Sweet with the odour of "codlins and cream."

II.

Such is my dream, be it other's possession,
Theirs be the real;
Mine the ideal;
So shall al move in Love's rhythmic procession.
Here, where the moor slowly slopes to the steam,
Taming its wildness to pastures that gleam
Under a dappled sky,
Fairy-spun mists go by
While, all unmoved, the great cloud- mountains dream.

III.

Sweet leafy wreathings;
Soft summer breathings,
  Breathings so human—
Tenderly human when nearest divine;
Pure love of man for pure love of woman
Showing us here, who have need of its shine,
  Just a faint glimpse ere it burst on us quite—
  Love's shoreless ocean of infinite light—
Past the earth-shadows that, lifting so slowly,
Veil with life's curtains the cloudless Most Holy,
  Till we can bear the ineffable sight.

IV.

Here, where the moor gathers purple each day,
Dyeing her vesture while sunsets delay,
Tenderly-hued, like a wind-ruffled feather
Peeps the grey rock from its garment of heather,
While, looking upward, the wistful-eyed land
Watches the clouds held as gifts in God's Hand.
Here the gorse-glory a burning bush shows,
Who lit he flame each true worshipper knows;
Here the glad wind sets the hare-bells a-swinging,
What if our ears are too dull for their ringing!
Well we know exquisite music is theirs—
Bells of His Temple that ring us to prayers.

V.

So we have soared somewhat high in our dream
(Holiday singers of holiday theme);
Let us come back to the side of the stream
  Where the gay fringe of its border is frayed;
  Where its full beauty emerges from shade
Fragrant and glorious with "codlins and cream."

July 23, 1890

A YEAR'S CHANGES

I.

He muttered, 'Just a year to-night—'
  Then silence. *Dead?* Beyond a doubt
With those faint words his soul went out
On other quest. I moved the light;
And closed the eye-lids, wonder-wide,
That had now secret now to hide,
  Nor any love, nor any hate,
  And then I sat to muse and wait—
"A year to-night," he said , and died.

II.

Then a kind-hearted woman came,
  With tenderness and homely grace
(Man's service is not quite the same),
  And straightened up the little place,
  And drew a sheet above the face.

III.

'Twas strange, before she came, to sit
Beside—shall I say *him* or *it?* —
  And feel that hands not mine, but hers,
  Must be his last ministers:
He, who helped many, helpless now,
  At least it seems so, it may be
  His energies at last are free
And we see but the placid brow,
While he, where sight no more is dim,
Sees and accepts our love for him,
And helps us still as he knows how.

IV.

Can we recall him, yet unhid
Beneath the jealous coffin-lid?
  Those keen grey eyes, whose glance you knew
  Saw in a moment false from true,
From whose clear deeps a soul most wise
Looked swiftly into other eyes;
  Your weakness saw, your goodness too,
  Saw all the best, the worst, of you;
Saw all, as one to seeing born
Shows no surprise nor any scorn
  But, looking through an atmosphere
  Where good and bad, alike, are clear,
Still firmly holds the weight of good
  Preponderates above the ill,
  And helps you thus your place to fill
By his belief in brotherhood.

V.

Not joyful he, nor scarcely gave,
  He simply walked in calmness past,
  As one whose self is anchored fast,
And yet can ride on any wave;
  Secure, yet not as those who bless
  Themselves in their self-consciousness,
But rather like a tree that grows
  And spreads abroad its summer shade,
  And loves the un, yet, undismayed,
Accepts the winds nor fears the snows.

VI.

Some secret had he! It may be;
But not for you and not for me
To search what is not freely shown;
If such he had, it was his own,
  And one's beside; we cannot tell.
We knew that tender smile, whose grace
Lies upon the quiet face,
  And calmly tells us all is well,
And while we count his sixty years,
We fail to know the countless tears,
That felt the magic of that spell,
And caught its sunlight ere they fell.

VII.

You *knew* him in some sort of way;
  I *loved* him, and I felt so small
  My love and knowledge were to all
His greater being; could I say
  That I had gauged that mighty soul,
  Or read the index of the whole
In glances that had merely played
  A moment, like swift gleams of light,
Upon the surface? He, Who made,
  And *one* He gave, alone could know,
  And she died just a year ago;
  Strange—just a year ago to-night.

THEO

Blue eyes 'neath a cotton bonnet!
  Theme for sweetest song or sonnet,
Could we find, by dwelling on it,
  Words in which to utter duly
  What those dear eyes tell us truly.

Blue eyes! could they e'er be bluer?
True eyes! could they e'er be truer?
Visions growing fainter, fewer!
  Or, perhaps the fault lies solely
  With our eyes that miss the lowly.

Little hands held out to reach me;
Baby lips that soft beseech me;
Words that sweet child-wisdom teach me,
  Gathered from some blest evangel
  Spoken by her holy Angel.

Human speech she yet is learning;
Human modes of thought discerning;
And her face reveals the burning
  Of some question, deep and tender,
  That our language fails to render.

And we love to think she knoweth
Wisdom such as God bestoweth,
Where His Tree-of-healing groweth;
  For those eager lips will flutter
  With the truths they cannot utter.

And we often wonder greatly,
When she folds her hands sedately,
Where she caught that manner stately—
  Wonder, till we feel quite certain
  'Twas the other side life's curtain.

When a trouble nears and presses
She would rout it with caresses;
Hide my face in sunlit tresses;
  And her laugh is softer, crisper,
  Than a bird's song or a whisper.

What a rain of treasure this is,
Falling in those baby kisses;
What a crowning bliss of blisses—
  But our eyes are often holden
  Where the wealth is spirit-golden.

Yet with all her nameless graces,
Sweetly human her sweet face is,
Where each smile its fellow chases;
  For the joyous soul within it
  Lets no other rest a minute.

Was she gift or have we won her,
With the bloom of heaven upon her,
Bringing earth celestial honour?
  Could our spirit's highest thrilling
  Ever claim such sweet fulfilling?
Gift is she and gifts she bringeth!

Music, when her laughter ringeth;
Sun-born song about her flingeth
  Such a zone of joy, we wonder
  By what name they know her yonder.

Here, we Theodora call her;
Can our love a moment thrall her?
For we fear her growing taller:
  We would have her woman, never,
  But a little child for ever.

And she tells us, little sleeper,
When she wakes, of pastures deeper
Than our meadow. Angels keep her
  In her dreams; all evils flee her,
  When *they* come from heaven to see her.

There, she says, she often wanders,
Fairy-led, or sits and ponders
Where a little stream meanders;
  For the child quite unaware is
  That the Angels are her fairies.

Should some real grief surprise her,
Trust and love within her eyes are;
And we know that she is wiser
  Than ourselves whose lives are shaded
  When *our* little hopes have faded.

Vanished dreams their gifts restore me;
Borne by tiny hands before me,
And a music rises o'er me,
  Never breathed in song or sonnet
  From beneath this summer bonnet.

SUN-STEEPED

Light upon all things, piercing through the shield
Of forest tracery to sombre paths
With living gold-shafts, touching fainting leaves
To seeming life and movement. Light, all light,
And heat and drought, and not a voice of bird,
Nor hum of insect: silently a flower
Slow falls from its high place to deck the earth:
Afar, a sound of water, ceaselessly,
Adown a channelled rock among the hills,
Making a wearying rhythm.

Cloudless skies,
Unvaried ever by a passing wing,
Or wandering mist; deep, clear, intensest blue,
Mingled with gold when, overhead, the car
Of the great sun-god, with its dazzling wheels,
Flames on half-blinded mortals who have dared
To face its glory with unveiléd eyes.
How all life fails in motion! here the snake
Flattens its listless folds; the reeking slime
Of that foul swamp is scarce more still than those
Huge lizards of its deeps that, log-like, float
In steaming tanks, and not an errant wind
Among the tree tops. Light a breathless heat;
And far things ever looking close at hand;
And painful silence, broken by the click
Of ripened vessels that release their seeds
From shrivelled keeping. Just one shadow, black

In sharpest contrast, on the yellow earth,
Falls straight beneath the palm-crown, where I lie
Wrapt from the glare, and, waking, dream my dream
Of other lands, far off, whose glory smote
My soul and left such memory as this:
Green earth, blue sky, grey water, purple hills,
And golden sun above them flooding all;
All, from topmost ridge of mountain pines,
Down to the fern's brown root in quiet combe
That drinks the sunlight through its feathery screen.
Light on the glacier on the mountain side
Flashed from a thousand facets and resolved
To hues prismatic, red and blue and gold:
Light on the lake that sleeps a league below.
Light on the golden furze and purple heath
And crimson foxgloves of far other hills;
Light on the trembling corn that clothes their base
With vesture changing in its living hues;
Light on the bird's plume and the insect's wing
That flash across the pathway of the sun;
And in my heart a sun that rises once,
Lord of no transient summer—Love's own light.

FAILURE?

You call this "failure", I, "success";
You think that he succumbed to death
 I, that he bowed before a wreath
Held out to crown him, nothing less.

"If he had striven he might have scaled,"
 You say, "the sunlit path of fame,
 And written high a fading name;
But this he did not and he failed."

I say, "He had not though to rise,
 But just to do; still less to treat
 His fallen fellows, at his feet,
As steps by which to reach a prize."

And yet about himself he drew
 A little circle, pure in soul;
 True units of as noble whole
That all unconscious lived and grew.

No party waited on his nod;
 Unchecked the tide of life will move;
 He gained and kept one woman's love
And the approval of his God.

'DOE YE NEXTE THYNGE'
(OLD SAXON LEGEND)

I have a song to sing,
  But how to sing it? Ah! these broken chords
Interpret all too well the faltering words,
That have no touch of Spring.

I have a tale to tell,
But how to hell it? All round is fair,
And birds with their love-stories fill the air;
With them all things are well.

I have a life to live,
But how to live it?
              "Life and song and tale
Flow from the nearest duty; none shall fail
Who give what they can give."

A WORD OF REMEMBRANCE

We sat between the cannons in the wind,
   That filled their empty, voiceless, throats with sound,
  And best with frozen breath against the hill;
Awhile it lulled and then, in fury blind,
  Caught up the maddened sleet and dashed it round
  The shiv'ring hawthorns and once more was still!
We heard it, yet we seemed to hear it not,
  Its troubled cry on other troubles fell
Unheeded; with clasped hands we sat and thought
  On tears we would not see, yet saw to well.
Oh helpless ones! but, even then your form
  Arose, endued with helpful pride, at length,
Clear-voiced, beneath the incoherent storm,
  You spoke such words as gird a man with strength.

MAY-DAY

Away
Clouds of the morning from the face of day!
  Let the glad earth again behold the sight,
  That fills her bosom with its throbbing light—
The birth of May.

Awake
O sleeping world, and bid the music break
  From wingèd choristers till grove and stream
  Unite, in varied strain, to hymn the theme,
For love's sweet sake!

Unfold
O leafy banners, and ye cups of gold
  Gather the dew-drops; flakes of living snow,
  That woo the sun, nor fear his generous glow'
Your Queen behold!

But let
Young human hearts acknowledge deeper debt,
  And, loyally responsive, soul and sense
  Vibrate to Eden's breath of eloquence,
That lingers yet.

Delay
No more: come song and dance, come mirth and play;
  Sound of glad insect; voice of lamb and bird;
  Come all things fair and joyous—in one word;
Come May.

IN KEMPSEY CHURCH

[In an arched niche, in the chancel wall of Kempsey church, is the tomb and recumbent armed effigy of Sir Edmund Wylde (*ob.* 1620); and, from behind, a small horse chestnut tree has grown, and for many years held aloft its summer plume of leaves above the monument.]

O chestnut in the chancel, there,
  Where slides the Severn's silent wave
  Above the warrior's peaceful grave
Thou spreadest summer garments fair!

Thou dost through changing seasons teach
  Of Death and Life, as thou canst feel,
  Born on the year's unpausing wheel,
Within thyself the power of each.

O living type of living faith;
  Corruption into glory grown;
  Thou holdest out a victor's crown—
Thy prize—to deck the goal of death;

Beauty for ashes, light for gloom,
  Thou typest; immortality
  Put on, when we shall pass, like thee,
The robbing-chamber of the tomb:

O living type of quickened flesh,
  Thou mockest feebly muttered faith
  And, leaping from the vaults of death,
Unfurlest bannered glories fresh!

Thou hast another voice that thrills
  What time the river murky grows
  With autumn rains, and early snows
Descend by night and touch the hills;

Thou feelest then the coming strife,
  And icy fingers chill thy crown,
  That bows its golden leafage down
Before the anguish of thy life;

Thou showest thus our day of grief,
  As thou hadst knowledge of it all,
  And lettest through the silence fall,
In shadow of the night, a leaf.

Approx. 1890

SONG

Love, it was sweet in morning glory;
   Sweet was it there in April's gleam,
Hearing each the old love story
   Borne on the ever-flowing stream;
Sweet was it hand-in-hand to go,
   Watching the ripples speeding nigh,
Only to gaze as the waters flow,
   Spoke of our love and glided by—
Scarce a word uttered—you and I
   Spoke the stream that murmured by.

O the joy of a cloudless noon!
   "Mine for aye!" and the music rang,
Clear from our lips ion the wind of June,
   Out from our hearts , as we talked and sang;
O the stream leapt and the air was gay,
   Filled with our passion, seeming so
One with ourselves that perfect day;
   Singing with us in ceaseless flow,
O how we spoke as our hearts beat high
   While the stream laughed as it gambolled by!

Love, it is sad in a fading meadow,
   Under the grey of an Autumn sky,
Feeling the touch of life's black shadow—
   Death should we call it, you and I?—
Walking alone, o how shall I bear it,
   All through the time of the falling leaves:
How the steam mourns as I pause to hear it,
   Passing the place of the gathered sheaves:
Yet a light falls ion the further shore,
   Resting and waiting for evermore.

Approx. 1889

A POOL IN A MEADOW

Pollard willows guard the place,
   Pond-weeds clothe it nearly over,
Save where, drawing back a space,
They the clear, black, secret face
   Of the silent pool uncover.

Round about it tangled bushes,
   Here and there a little parted,
And, beneath them, tufts of rushes,
Where the moor-hen shyly pushes
   Into darkness when upstarted.

Solemnly the moon looks down
   She, I think, its secret guesses,
But the laughter-loving sun
Fain would such a hollow shun
   And avoids those drear recesses.

Wild fowl come across at night,
   Drop their quiv'ring feet within it,
Seek its shadows out of sight;
Leave it with the dawning light;
   But it knows nor thrush nor linnet:

Not a happy singing bird
  Ever wakes a note anear it;
Coots (with cry like human word,
Wrung from lips by anguish stirred)
  Know its deeps, but song birds fear it.

Once I heard a nightingale
  When the April dusk was looming,
Utter one long plaintive wail,
Then he hushed th' unspoken tale,
  Nevermore the strain resuming.

Now and then a purr will come
  While the night-jar hunts in shadow
Or the beetle's drowsy hum
(Like the boom of muffled drum)
  Reach from summer meadow.

Dead, upon the bottom there
  Lie the leaves of past Novembers;
Wealth of priceless colour rare.
Crimson, gold, all tincture fair,
  Blackened like the morrow's embers.

Yet the gloom had power to hold me
  And my steps, unconscious, tended
Where the mystery would enfold me,
And I knew, ere others told me,
  This was where a life had ended.

June 1889

A WORD UNSAID

A word unsaid: how many a word
  I've wished unspoken, but alas!
    This grieves me most—a good let pass.
Our eyes had met; your check averred
Love's rich pulsations there, and yet
The moment came; the moment fled;
And all my life I must regret
A word unsaid.

A word unsaid still follows me,
  Relentless, with its voiceless speech,
    "Too late, the good is past thy reach,"
So ever runs the comment free:
And friends, who learn half-truths, conclude
  That swift-born love was swiftly dead,
Nor dream there came in quietude
A word unsaid:

A word unsaid, whose message low
  No silence broke, but made it more;
    And were we *two* have walked before
One, only, sees a mound of snow;
Yet when we meet our souls will trace
  Their steadfast loves, though years have sped,
And I shall utter, face to face,
A word unsaid.

DARKNESS AND LIGHT

I.

Light? O my soul
  Is this the light,
That marks the longed-for goal;
  That crowns the height?

Why is this gloom;
  No sunbeams fall;
The shadows of that room
  Reserved for all.

So I have striven,
  To find at last
The summit-clouds unriven;
  The dark unpassed.

Beneath me now
  (With night around,
The herbless mountain's brow,
  For vantage ground)

Lie wasted years;
  And, O my soul,
Thou knowest many tears
  Have hid the goal

From blinded eyes,
  That strive in vain
To see, where shadow lies,
  The sun again.

And some have said,
  (Falsely, my soul)
Light binds about thy head
  "Its aureole:"

But well I know,
  God's face withdrawn
The gloom replaces glow,
  The darkness, dawn.

II.

Darkness? Nay light!
It may be dark without me, but within
I feel the morning of a day begin
That has no night.

Death, is it friend?
I cannot tell, it may be, but it seems
To me a waking, after fever-dreams
Have reached an end,

I think to-day
(Night is it? O my soul, it is not night
But day-break) first the life-long looked-for light
Upon my way,

Projects and falls
On cloud, that melts not but reforms and shows,
To fence the pathway that between it goes,
Its shining walls.

I, having trod
Life's dubious way, with firmer footsteps move:
This, which you call the "vale of Death" may prove
The mount of God.

At last I see
(How have I waited!) God, that in Thy sight
The darkness is no darkness—dark and light
Are like to Thee.

SONNETS OF THE SEASONS

Spring

I. THE PROMISE

Still lingers in the furrow, running down
  The mountain's face, a streak of Winter's snow,
  Unwilling, yet, with feeble tears to go
From where it long has lain. The hoary crown
The sun has filched, and sorrow's token drown
  A chastened beauty, yet the Earth shall show
  A fairer sight when all her flowers blow
Beneath the smile that follows on the frown.
Joy after sorrow; gloom that brightness shuns;
  Life after death and motion after pause;
Returning vigour with returning suns;
  Hope rising, quickened by undying laws,
Still witness to a deathless, sleepless Cause
  Controlling ever—so their message runs.

II. GRADUAL SPRING

Bird voices gather volume day by day
  Where wind-flowers whiten under naked boughs,
  The trusted confidants of early vows
And nesting schemes. Here a precious spray,
Leafless and black, with crowded bloom is gay:
  In that warm nook the Celandine allows
  Her golden stars to glisten: now endows,
The Primrose, with pale gold, each woody way.
Skies of intenser blue provoke earth's green,
  In loving rivalry, to clothe her woods:
  The hedgerows brighten with their leafy buds
Ere yet the Hawthorn's snowy wreath is seen:
  Now anxious parent birds and clamant broods
Declare that Winter is not, but *has been*.

III. THE COMING OF SPRING, 1889

Blue, green and such a stream of shifting gold
  And softest shadow, falling everywhere
  And not abiding; palpitating air,
And hum of life from voices manifold
Fused in one paean, hinting things untold,
  Unframed by those lips even, trembling there
  Beneath the gleaming eyes and rippling hair,
Of her whose love has touched the sullen cold.
I lay in dreamless sleep; my blood was dull
  With that drear influence, which surely numbs,
  Of Winter long protracted, week on week—
And Spring was here, my sweet bride-beautiful:
  She came, as one on tip-toe softly comes,
  And woke me with a kiss on either cheek.

Summer

I. JUNE 1889

Summer at last: the cloudless skies of noon;
  The birds' full carol and the fragrant breeze
  Filled with the drowsy hum of wakeful bees!
How sadly must the heart be out of tune
That finds no music in the songs of June,
  Nor catches, when the west-wind takes the trees,
  The undertone of angel-melodies
That cross our lives and leaves us all too soon!
So some loved presences, low voices, come
 About our pathway, brighten us, and cease;
    Say, do the leave us lonelier than before?
    Not so, for their sweet memory evermore
 Is like a message from the haunts of peace,
"Your feet are also surely nearing home."

II. COMBAT

Here to the wayside thistle flashing down,
  Like flakes of Heaven's own blue, the butterflies
  Unfurl their wings across the purple dyes,
Or lift them and reveal soft grey and brown:
In hot haste now (but shall he win renown?)
  Another claimant, fiery-vested, hies
  In burnished red, with half-a-hundred eyes,
And combat ranges o'er the thistle's crown.
What lesson? Surely none, yet would we gaze
  On life and beauty while the seasons roll,
And watch sweet Nature's doings, learn her ways
  Look on the workings of her mighty soul,
  So woo some secret from the hidden whole,
And then be thankful for the summer days.

III. A SUMMER DAY*

Lo! twice to-day God touched His heaven with flame,
   And who regarded? At the early break
   He scattered golden wealth o'er sky and lake
In boundless affluence; when evening came
He traced the mystery of His awful Name
   In fiery characters, and many a flake
   Of crimson, where the pillared poplars shake
Black in the west, and so His light proclaim.
So God bestows, and we accept His light
   And barely marvel—'tis a common thing—
Or, looking lightly, soon forget it quite—
   A sunbeam glancing from a swallow's wing—
Nor heed His witness, set 'twixt night and night,
   To love that should not need witnessing.

---

* [Editor's note: Reprinted, to complete this series, from "A Life, Love and other Poems."]

Autumn

I. THE YEAR'S WEALTH

The elms are clad in triumph-robes of gold,
  And orchards glowing in autumnal blaze,
  Lifted from Earth to Heaven through dark'ning days
Flushed with a flame which they alone behold;
Gathered and stored, while seasons slowly rolled
  Through that half-cycle, since the first love-lays
  Of mating birds filled all the wooded ways
With promise, till the gorse lit up the world.
Dear Earth! when Spring's new garments greet the sky
  How fair is her awaking—green, beneath
The snow-fringed blue of April's canopy—
  Still lovely through all growth, till that first wreath
Is turned to gold by true life's alchemy;
  Most glorious in the vestments of her death.

II. FULFILMENT

I think Earth's glory consummates to-day,
  And, like a gift, upon her altar lies:
  There falls the flame-shaft on her sacrifice,
A sight to dream of when the heavens are grey.
The Swallow-armies still their flight delay
  And form in broken lines. Approving skies
  O'er-arch the splendour of these nameless dyes,
Sun-mingled—Earth's last effortless display.
A sight to dream of; to fulfil desire;
  Seen, life's assured possession: Earth reveals,
    Once in the perfect circle of the year,
    Herself in passion and when gloom is here,
  Or Winter's shroud across her bosom steals,
We know, beneath, she has a heart of fire.

III. DISAPPOINTMENT

Strange that accomplishment should balk desire;
  Full hand bring emptied hopes and doubtful gain;
  Fulfilment, with a sorrow in its train,
Robs aspiration of its vital fire:
Flushed brows, ere scarcely crowned, of kingship tire,
  And pleasure comes and, coming, turns to pain:
  Less sad it is to seek than to obtain:
Want, not success, must restless souls inspire.
Spring's promise, Summer's progress—and the end
  Satiety not satisfaction! Why
Can we not take the gifts the Seasons send
By their gift-bearer, Autumn? Must we cry
(In longing or regret our peace expend),
"I would possess" possessing, "I would die"?

October 1889

Winter – Three Aspects

I. GLOOM

From park and hedgerow leaf-stripped arms arise
  To these unanswering heavens in mute appeal
    Born of bereavement; clouds, scarce-cleft, reveal
A pale, unsympathetic light that lies
Across the frozen earth and feebly dies
  Before the early darkness. All things feel
    A touch of nearing death upon them steal
And know the lordship of the sunless skies.
Is it for those leafy coronals
   Were twined? For this, o'er laid with Autumn's gold,
     Earth's richest garments spread to deck the year?
And comes no answer from the curtained halls,
    No warm smile on these dead leaves lying here,
  Toys of all winds, first victims of the cold?

II. BEAUTY

Skies blue as Summer's; clouds a fleecy white;
  (Snow-coated icebergs sailing northern seas
   In silent majesty and native ease
And calm progression of self-conscious might)
Such hath this winter day to show, and bright,
  On hoar-crowned hills and lines of traceried trees,
   The sunbeams come with Summer memories
And fill the present with a past delight.
Thou, Winter, hast a beauty all thine own;
  These fallen leaves fresh vistas bring to view
And open up the charm, before unknown,
   Of deep-bowered homesteads peeping coyly through
Wood-spaces where a veil had round them grown,
  Hiding a loveliness the song-birds knew.

III. RESTING IN HOPE

Asleep, beneath her snowy coverlid,
  Our weary Earth accepts the priceless boon
  Of rest and silence, while the patient moon
Keeps the night watches—all her beauty hid,
As all her scars—ah! who shall her forbid
  The heavy sleep of an unbroken swoon
  While change the years? They shall the summer noon
Know once again life that nigh has slid.
So comes the rest of death to crown the strife
  Of weary souls, unconquered, yet. So glad
    To creep within the shadow and to lie
    Awaiting, while the dark days pass them by
  With quiet tread. Sweet it is, and not sad,
This pause between the mighty years of life.

December 1889

TO THE AUTHOR OF "EMPIRE"

Sweet singer, from thy home of cloudless skies,
  Thou bringest sunshine to this gloom of ours:
  The month with thee is always one of flowers,
And every sound has secret harmonies:
Thou findest beauty ever, with clear eyes
  That look beyond the veil of cloud that lowers
  Between us and the sun: we know thy powers
That find the death less when the mortal dies.
Shall we thy lesson miss and do the wrong?
  Dream thy true life has been a sunlit plain
  Of joyance? rather in the paths of pain
Dost thou find sunshine; passing so along
  The vale of Baca, drought for thee is rain:
Thy stricken soul gives her response in song.

ON GUSTAV DORE'S PICTURE, "*PAOLO AND FRANCESCA DI RIMINI*"

O pierced ones! still to th' undying death
  So faithful. Floating o'er the molten flood,
Ye seem as damnèd angels, whom the breath
  Of heaven yet clings to, marred with lust and blood,
So faithful is your sin! No passions await
  To break the fixed despair: to well ye know
The dread inscription o'er the Infernal gate,
  "Through me ye enter the abode of woe."
O helpless agony! So false, so true!
  O pierced frail ones! I could well-nigh weep
To see your grief, yet ye bring comfort too;
  How high may love be, since ye show how deep!
This hope I bear, Francesca, past the door;
Those eyes of thine are on me evermore!

October 11th, 1870

ON MALVERN HILLS

I stand on these plutonic rocks and read
  The record of Earth's fury at my feet,
  What time she rent herself in fervent heat
Of self-asserting anger and decreed
Her waters' limit. Now the fiery deed
  She covers with a vesture; mosses sweet,
  And timid hare-bells, bolder foxgloves meet
And deck her scars where sheep in quiet feed.
Thus our Earth-mother, feared, misunderstood,
  Works out her children's welfare through her pain,
Then gives a peaceful bosom to her brood
  And stores their garners with all precious grain,
And we—we love her best in gracious mood
  And know her our true mother once again.

June 11, 1889

A SHELTER

Love, you remember when that summer breeze
  Bore the white fleeces on their silent chase
  Across the sky, athwart the moon's fair face,
(Yet lovelier when looking out behind
Those webs of gossamer than unconfined
  By any trammels in her nightly race).
  A calm hill-hollow held us in its place
Of shelter, yet by moonlight undivined,
The world lay all beneath us lapped in light,
  Ourselves untouched, the breezes past us swept;
More beautiful than any day was night,
  We could, well-nigh, for want of speech have wept,
Who, out or narrowing shadow, watched the sight
  As on from rock to rock the moon-wave crept.

MUTABILITY

A sky cloud-fleeced at sunset, every flake
  Blushing to softest red from feather-white
  In sweet gradation, just a parting sight
Of rosy islands in a sapphire lake:
Child-voices full of mirth for Summer's sake,
  Who gives the merry hay-fields and the light
  Of longest ev'nings: slowly comes the night
To days and hearts that gladly brightness take.
The eye was satisfied with colour; sound
  Of living music came the ear to fill,
And, while delight did wholly wrap me round,
  I knew no sense of any loss nor ill,
But deemed myself possessing, till I found
  The sky was grey and those child-voices still.

SOLITUDE

"We die alone." Ah, yes! but more than this,
  Alone we live; our life's full-motioned tide
  Sways to the forces that its progress guide,
By trackless ways, across its *own* abyss.
Alone, we know of anguish and of bliss,
  And, walking reverently at Nature's side,
  Behold the beauty of the mother-bride
Who seals our consecration with her kiss.
Alone the hidden path by each is trod;
  Man moves amid his fellows, but his soul
    Scales heights where not another soul has been;
    Seeks the untrodden; searches the unseen—
  Itself a part of the Eternal Whole—
Alone with Nature and alone with God.

June 1889

OUT OF THE PAST

A stretch of common and, beyond, the hills;
  About their feet a narrow belt of trees,
  Like children climbing to their parents' knees
In love's disorder of untutored wills:
Such is the picture that my memory fills
  From her sweet store of treasured images;
  And, from the lime-tops, comes the hum of bees
On fragrant breathings that the morn distils.
A moment since life's rush and whirl were here,
  And I was bowed before them, now, I seem
  To move beneath the influence of a dream
In which the past, once more, is showing clear,
  Undimmed by distance, and the tender gleam
Of eyes, long closed to me, again is near.

THE HEART AND THE TREASURE

Here with my face to heaven (the meadow-grass
  A waving forest seems) content I lie:
  Above the great cloud-argosies go by,
Like white souls moving on a sea of glass;
They come in silence, each resistless mass
  Cleaves trackless heights, while bound to earth am I,
  Who greet them, watch them sail the summer sky,
And feel their shadows as they onward pass.
Here, sounds of birds and insects reach me; there,
I see their mazy dances in the air,
  And falls upon my face the flower's sweet breath;
Fair sights may go, fair memories remain,
And Love will count her treasure o'er again,
  Sure it awaits her past the seas of Death.

HUMAN INABILITY (ON SOME ATTEMPTED STATEMENTS OF TRUTH)

All mingled, Nature's hues result in light;
  But when we try her message to translate
  We mix our pigments with another fate
And darkness follows when they so unite;
Too gross our colours and too dull our sight;
  Unskilled our treatment; how should we create
  Pure things from things impure? we must await
The school of Paradise to teach us right.
So when we analyse, to recombine,
  Th' eternal truth of God, our efforts rude
  Fail in its presentation; cold and crude,
They miss the vital principle, its sign
  And secret force; too often unimbued
Is our divinity with the Divine.

VEILED

I know not any man who, looking back,
  Says, "I would walk the self-same way again
  That I have travelled—where it lies so plain
What need of change?" Ah, no! the backward track
Shows strange and tortuous, shadows, over-black,
  Fall on it and our feet would shrink the pain
  Of thorns that pierce, and stones that bruise, and rain
Of tears that blind and make our footsteps slack.
Our way was possible, because we trod
  Unknowing what its length and where its end,
    And hidden joy was there, as hidden grief—
    But Thou, who knowest were it long or brief
  And saw the course our faltering steps would tend,
Veiled all the path. For this we thank Thee, God.

June 1889

UNVEILED

The breath of lime-trees reached me, odorous
  With summer sweetness: softly musical
  Bee-murmurs came. I looked, a heavy wall
Rose in red blankness there, calamitous
To dreams of leafage, hung with pendulous
  Gold blossoms that, with gentle rise and fall,
  Marked wingèd visitants. Swift vanished all
The vision, that a moment held me, thus.
So sometimes, spirit-quickened, we may see
  The other side of Death's wall—a touch of air
Blows on us and the fair twelve-fruited tree
  Shows by the river; then we are aware
Of mortal limitations, yet are free
  To *know* Heaven's tree, as Earth's, is surely there.

A MAN

Most courteous was he, generous to those
  Who thought not with him: most intolerant
  Of pampered vice, whose sway was dominant,
And unrebuked held court; for this arose
The clear decisive protest, such as shows
  No hope of compromise; no low-voiced cant
  Sullied his speech, nor any soulless rant
Of surface passion, aping vital throes.
Skilful to find the man beneath the creed,
  Such was he; one you looked upon and loved
Just for his self's sake, paying little heed
  What vesture wrapped the soul, whose motions moved
  You to responsive action and disproved
All charge of narrowness by amplest deed.

ANOTHER MAN

Stained with the hue of toil and graved by care;
  At times relaxing to expression dull,
  Beneath the press of labour; beautiful
When looking on a child, as one aware
Of some diviner presence, that might share
  The child presentment and so disannul
  Material pleadings and infuse the lull
Of toil-born apathy with quick'ning air.
Hard-handed and rough voiced, your instinct found
  A latent passion thrilled him when he spoke
In praise or censure, and you felt the round
  Of duty might some sternest deed invoke:
  Rugged his aspect, as his country's oak,
Which breasts the wind, and with a heart as sound.

A WOMAN

Strong in the woman-strength whose name is Love;
  Weak in the confidence that stands alone,
  Regardless of all rights it tramples on;
Strong in reliance, and how strong to move
To vaster effort trusted souls can prove,
  Won form themselves, to higher duties won,
  By just the woman's need a moment shown
In tenderness with child-like faith inwove.
Such was she, and we never thought her great;
  We loved her, that was all, our eyes were sealed;
    The herald, Death, proclaims her place at length.
Did this new rank surprise her; she, who late
  Scarce noticed moved among us? Now revealed,
    Where seeming weakness is transformed to strength.

AN IDEAL

Not beautiful, as some count beauty, yet
  To me so fair: the symbol of a soul
  Expressed most clearly by the perfect whole
Of face and form and motion : I forget,
In that sweet presence, stricter canons set
  Of loveliness, and gladly pay the toll
  Of vanquished spirits. Hers the love-changed pole
To which the heart turns ere the eyes have met.
Not one love is for her—the love of all
  Is tendered loyally and rough hearts greet
  Her coming; wan-faced children of the street
Lookup and feel such sunshine lightly fall
As makes some common day a festival,
  Marked by the passing of those gentle feet.

Approx. 1890

DEVELOPMENT

As I have seen develop a fair face
  Beneath Time's moulding finger, touching light
  Each plastic feature, until human sight
Can long no more for any added grace;
So I have seen and loved a soul to trace
  Through its increasing beauty—Day and Night
  Bringing their tribute to an infinite
Supremacy, whose realm is not of space.
And I have seen the victor soul possess
  Itself of that flesh-fairness and present
  To us its very self's embodiment
(Which yet than its essential self is less)
  Till, to the calm of a complete content,
Sinks satisfied our want-born restlessness.

November 1891

UNSPEAKABLE

All nature strives to find the fittest word
   By which t'express Thee: sometimes human speech
   Plays on the confines of those truths that reach
Beyond all voice, all thought; at times a chord
Is touched by sound or colour—song of bird
   Or hue of sky or flower, rendering each
   Its tribute to that knowledge none may teach
In fullness—impotent to name Thee, Lord.
Thou dost in all Thy works Thyself reveal,
   But all Thy works can only feebly trace,
     In rudest character for eyes like ours
      Their message; and these finite, infant powers
   Read it but dimly. When we see Thy face
That which no word can name our souls will feel.

Trinity Sunday 1889

ON RUTHLESS EXPLORATION

We pray for light, but let the light be Thine;
  Hell-streaks, fiend-fingers with mad glee might trace
  In fire and blood across Night's shuddering face,
We see enough of; let Thy true Light shine!
Must it be so, the pioneer's red line
  And cursed memory, deathless in disgrace,
  Shall mark the advent of the stronger race,
That claims by might alone a right divine?
Must each new passage prove a locust flight
  And leave a blasted land? O Judge on high,
  Beholding where Thy stricken children lie,
Whose blood is ever precious in Thy sight,
  Forgive us if, with shaken faith, we cry
For darkness rather than such lurid light.

"MISSED HIS VOCATION"
(A disputed Verdict)

"Missed his vocation," say you? It may be
  That God sees otherwise, beholding all,
  And knowing how he answered to the call,
And, with no murmur, live the life we see:
Not dignified, nor even scarcely free
  Enough to catch a breathing interval
  Between the shadow's lifting and its fall,
When wary limbs obey the night's decree.
I think he has not missed it; some are glad
  And all are better for the life he lived:
  It seemed he gave out more than he received
And brightened others when himself was sad.
I think God, who a wider sphere forbad,
  Will hold his failure as work achieved.

LOSSES

Lost coin, lost sheep, lost son—for these we seek,
  And scatter strength in fretting, helplessly;
  But Thy search, Lord, can never fruitless be,
And Thy strength faileth not to lift the weak
Who turn their faces toward that tender steak
  Of light that touches them and heralds Thee
  (Whose nearer presence helps dim eyes to see
And whose low whisper prompts dumb lips to speak).
Lord shall we find our treasures yet again
  In Thy vast store of lost things, gathered there
From all dark places where *we* looked in vain,
  With eyes so full of tears and hearts of care? —
But Thou, Who knowest our exceeding pain,
  Dost this exceeding joy, I think, prepare.

SATISFIED

I saw a little baby-child to-day,
  So still and silent; but a week ago
  Her cheek was flushed where now no colours flow
In subtle changes: whispers, voiceless, say
"Be still, be humble, ye whose heads are grey
  As children are before her—she must know
  What ye have failed in guessing—swiftly, so,
She passed to wisdom from her simple play."
I cannot think "In Death's embrace she lies,"
  Her quiet has no touch of strange alarms,
I, rather, looks on those close-lidded eyes
  As closed to all environment of harms,
As seeing that which wholly satisfies—
  God's likeness—waking in th' Eternal Arms.*

---

* cf Wisdom of Solomon iv. 13 ; psalm xvii 15

SLEEP

Man to his labour, till the shadows come
   And bear on silent wings God's gift of sleep,
   Goeth from day to day, to sow; to reap;
Or bear, at length, the gathered harvest home:
And, in the city's heart, the chattering loom
   Is checked in utterance, and the mighty leap
   Of iron pulses stilled, and stayed the sweep
Of enginery beneath the touch of gloom.
So, when that greater day has ceased its roar,
   And through the dirge, we catch the distant psalm,
And on the threshold of Life's awful door,
   The thorn-branch laid, ere yet is grasped the palm,
They fold their hands from labour evermore
   And His beloved sleep in restful calm.

Malvern Parish Magazine, March 1892

NEW POEMS.

We commend to our readers the new volume of poetry, "A Garden and Other Poems," by our neighbour, Mr. R. F. Towndrow, who is already well known as a graceful and sympathetic poet. His new volume is well worthy of the author and of its predecessor.

"Northern Daily News," Feb 15/92

IN A GARDEN, AND OTHER POEMS. By Richard Francis Towndrow. (London: T. Fisher Unwin.)

This is another dainty little volume of poems, with a very attractive exterior, to which, in a literary sense, much that is inside corresponds. The author published a former volume, entitled "A Life, Love, and other Poems," and was so encouraged by the reception it received that he has been tempted to make a second venture. The verses are simple in their composition, and of varying merit, but there are some genuine strains of heart music amongst them. The first poem, "A Garden," has a very tuneful lilt in its verse. Here is a stanza or two :—

> The years have hid the garden,
>   Whose lichen-painted door
> The child would often enter,
>   On sunny days of yore;
> In vain, it seems, to find it,
>   I search for evermore.
>
> At times amid the shadow,
>   At times amid the gleam,
> Again I see the garden,
>   Like some familiar dream,
> Where real things seem visions,
>   And visions real seem.
>
> Sometimes a breath of lilies,
>   From a basket in the street,
> And a weary face above them,
>   Will speak of weary feet
> That wandered in the garden
>   'Mid the odour and the heat.

"An Artist's Ideal," "A Year's Changes," "Theo," "Darkness and Light," are among the best of the poems, though some of the nature pictures and the sonnets, of which there is a considerable number, are also of much merit. Generally this versifier's notes are in the minor key, as though life's sadness and sorrow oppressed his muse, but the pathos is natural and pleasing, and enlivened with touches of gaiety.

"Manchester Guardian," Feb 24/92

Mr. Towndrow's verses are altogether on a higher plane. They attain the interesting, especially in a sort of irregular rondeau entitled "The Word Unsaid", and in some sonnets; nor can they be ever fairly said to be merely trivial and slovenly. But in virtue of these very merits they must needs be subjected to a different and higher test—the test of distinction; and here, we are afraid, they fail. There is scarcely a piece among them that "a Christian or an ordinary man" need be actually ashamed to have written; hardly one, either, that a critical Christian or a wise ordinary man would particularly plume himself on. It should be observed that Mr. Towndrow handles the "In Memoriam" stanza with some skill.

"Bradford Observer," Feb 17/92

Somewhat nearer the mark, but not very much, stand some verses by Richard F. Towndrow, called "A Garden and other Poems" (T. Fisher Unwin). An unpruned, unreal fancy has dictated many of these verses. Sound and fury, signifying nothing, may fairly describe some of them. Addressing a horse-chestnut that grows out of an ancient tomb, Mr. Towndrow bursts out thus :—

> Beauty for ashes, light for gloom,
>   Thou typest; immortality
> Put on, when we shall pass, like thee,
>   The robing-chamber of the tomb.

What does it all mean?

"Saturday Review," March 19/92

More decorous and more dull are the contents of Mr. Towndrow's little book of fluent and harmless verse. Observation they show of the external facts that a country ramble affords—the "dead pieces of Nature," as Addison says—and it is accurate, though not deep, and invariably unimaginative. So, in other ways, the surface of things is just brushed, and a pretty ripple of verse flows, not unpleasing, but in nowise moving. The sonnets, of which there are thirty at least, are laboured and inexpressive. The rhymes of them strike the ear like ringing blows on an anvil, thus :—

> Most courteous was he; generous to those
>   Who thought not with him; most intolerant
>   Of pampered vice, whose sway was dominant,
> And unrebuked held court; &c.

A Man.

Most courteous was he, generous to those
 Who thought not with him: most intolerant
Of pampered vice, whose sway was dominant,
And unrebuked held court; for this alone
The clear decisive protest, such as shows
 No hope of compromise; no low-voiced cant
Sullied his speech, nor any smallest vaunt
Of surface passion, aping vital throes.
Skilful to find the man beneath the creed,
 Such was he; one you looked upon and loved
Just for his self's sake, paying little heed
What vesture wrapped the soul, whose motion, nerved
You to responsive action and disproved
All charge of narrowness by amplest deed

Richard F. Towndrow

Section 3

Reproduction from

Sonnets Of Love, Life, and Death

(Originally published in 1896)

A REFUTATION

Dear, when you held the chalice of your love
  Against these lips, though scarce the faithless cry,
  "Love is no more!" had left them, straight was I
Low stricken by a power I would disprove.
  "Love is no more" I said. "Shall planets move,"
  Such seemed your answer, "while the ages fly
  "In pauseless cycles and Love, lifeless, lie,
"Defeated by the souls for whom he strove?"
My cry was like the joyless laughter heard
  Beneath the blear lamps: your answer came
Clear as the morning paean of a bird
  Whose soul goes forth in music's living flame
To greet its Giver.   So the clouds were stirred
  About God's feet. His love was still the same.

LOVE'S CONQUEST

Because you saved my soul with one slow kiss,
  Laid on my forehead, when the sun was down
  And the moon rose not—fearing not the frown
Of women nor man's smile—for this, and this
That your soft hair touched mine, and all th' abyss,
  Flushed like a snowy mountain's morning crown,
  Seen from the ruins of a rifled town
Where phantom's walk—for that new dawn of bliss—
When friends await the shadow of a wing
  To silence all, while yet the fluttering breath
  Proclaims you with them; when they
                    watch the strife
You wage alone—
Because you did this thing,
  May God's strong angel take the guise of Death
    And print upon *your* lips his kiss of life.

A JOURNEY

I.

A hand was laid upon me: in my dream
  Strange courage came, though neither form nor face
  The darkness yielded from its close embrace;
Then I was conscious of a might stream
Moaning beside me, and the stifled scream
  Of reeds, wind-tortured. With relentless pace,
  Our footsteps bore us ever from the place
Where wholly failed the light's last dying gleam.
Far off a sound, that might be human tears,
  In the wind-pauses, when the reeds were still,
Slow-dropping, fell upon my quickened ears,
And then I questioned (all bereft of fears)
  The name and end of that resistless Will,
And won for answer, "When the shadow clears."

II.

A rush of wings like passing wild-fowl, stirred
  The air to quick vibration, and the cry
  Of eager creatures, 'twixt the earth and sky,
Broke on us as a new-created word,
  Great with half-apprehended meanings, heard
  For the first time. A sense of freedom nigh
  Filled my caged spirit with pulsations, high
As the heart-beatings of a loosened bird.
Then first I knew my hand with tears was wet,
  "The way is long and they are still undried!"
My heart rebuked me, "Shall Love soon forget?"
  And, from that Presence ever at my side,
An answer came to words unframed as yet,
  "With dawn thy longing will be satisfied."

III.

The river's voice was changed; I knew a sea,
  That had no further shore, had hushed its moan
  With a great lullaby; so I have known
A child's cry to its mother's song agree,
And out of discord issue harmony.
  Then were the first fine airs of morning blown
  And reached us through the darkness, where alone
We stood with faces to infinity.
Then spread the dawn across the sea and land
  And, turning swiftly, I, with hurried breath,
    Looked in that face the night no more could hide,
    "I know you, LIFE!" exultingly, I cried,
  But he made answer, "*Others call me* DEATH"—
Waking, Love's tears were still upon my hand.

LOVE'S CRY

If ever I should spread my arms in vain,
  Mocked by the mirage of departed years,
  And sudden rapture turn to sodden tears,
And lips, unmated, piteously complain;
Let not her peace be broken by my pain,
  Nor loss be loss, where she, amid her peers,
  A music born of silence ever hears
In valleys where lost sunsets long have lain.

Love, thou hast helped me in the years gone by!
  How shall I help thee in the days that are?
May God transmute to prayer each wailing cry,
  And grief as gladness reach thee from afar;
  Till falls the earthward shadow of thy star
And, in its folds, I know that thou art nigh.

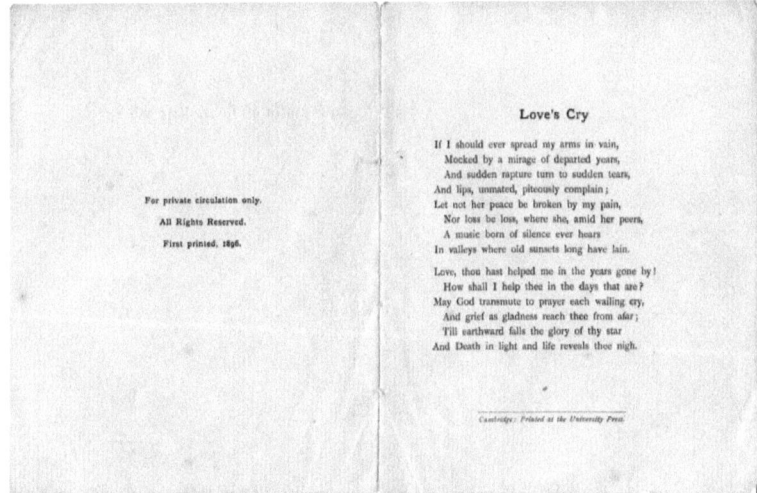

Section 4

Rare & Unpublished Poems

YOU AND I

We met before Death's trysting gate,
   Whose lives through all their course had drawn
To this ; we had not long to wait –
   Wan watchers for the dawn.

Like flutings from awakened birds
   At day-break in a belt of trees
Came music, fraught with mystic words
   More strange, more sweet, than these.

And we had met, to whom the past
   Showed one long love-with-duty strife ;
Together it was ours at last
   To leave and enter life.

So seemed it, God willed otherwise,
   For then (once more a parting , dear!)
Alone you entered Paradise
   And I am waiting here.

Malvern Link, March 1895

SPRING: A DREAM FULFILLED

Again we wait thy coming: through the drear,
Long nights and meagre days we dream of thee,
And think thee near when thou art far away,
And watch the herald buds on bush on tree
Unfold, ere yet thy footsteps touch the earth.

Spring with the willow-blossoms in her hair,
And wind-flowers on her bosom – snow to snow –
Spring with the celandine to star her path;
The blue-bell and the primrose in her train,
And subtle scent of hidden violets
Moving before her!

Thus we dream of thee.
And, while we dream, the hollows of the hills
Grow fair with March-born daffodils ,that light
Their shadows with faint flame at earliest dawn.
Below, the flocks are stirring, eager lambs
Utter that needful cry which, everywhere,
Quickens the mother's heart and saves the world.

The youth and love and beauty of the earth
We greet in thee, and sunnier climes send forth
Their swift-winged minstrels over land and sea
To hymn thy progress.
Overhead, the clouds
Sail their blue ocean in white majesty
And shadow chases shadow on the grass.

Now moves the new wine through the veins of earth,
And all the air is tremulous with wings
And flash and hum of myriad-moving life.
At last the mill-pond, willow-watched in sleep,
Wakes with a smile, as our first swallow's wing
Brushes its cheek in passing –
Start no more
We dream about thy coming. Thou art here.

April 1898

A GLASTONBURY THORN
(Flowering in the garden of the Swan Inn, Newland, Worcestershire, on Christmas Day 1903)

"Blossoms at Christmas, mindful of our Lord" –
    Thus he, whose song brought back the mystic Grail
    And Galahad and Bors and Percivale,
Of Glastonbury's Thorn. To me, the word
Tells of this tree, which through the year has stored
    Its fragrance for a gift, now skies are pale
    And leaves have fall'n, and summer blossoms fail
To deck the manger and their sweets afford.
    Here, in the garden of this village Inn,
    As there, beneath those Abbey walls, the flowers
        Open their treasures. At the Birthday Feast
Shall we be shamed? Can we no beauty win?
    No frankincense distil from sunnier hours
        To lay beside this offering of the East?

NOTE. – Joseph of Arimathea, so runs the legend, landed in Britain, and walked towards Glastonbury, where he afterwards founded the Abbey. Tired with their journey, the party rested at the place now called Weary-all-Hill; and Joseph struck his hawthorn staff in the ground; this grew and budded, blossoming at Christmas time.
The original tree has long since disappeared, but many cuttings were taken, and many places now possess a "Glastonbury Thorn."
It is mentioned in Tennyson's "Holy Grail", from which the first line of the above sonnet is taken.

AN EVENING HYMN

Again, dear Lord, our hymn of praise
   We lift to Thee, who givest all;
For Thy pure gift of nights and days
   We thank Thee and before thee fall:
Thou, Lord of darkness and of light,
Be with us through the nearing night.

Thou, in our pleasure, rest and toil,
   Has kept us while the hours have sped;
Let not our sins Thy mercies soil;
   Bid Thy good Angels guard our bed:
Dear Lord, when Thou withdrawest light,
Grant us Thy boon of sleep tonight.

We will not dread the dark for lo!
   No ill can harm whom Thou dost keep:
Fearless with had in Thine, we go
   Along the border-land of sleep;
Thy wings, O Lord, have veiled the light,
Their shadow is the blessèd night.

O Christ, to whom the glow, the gloom
   Of light and darkness are as one;
Who, form the portal of the tomb
   Came, heeding not the seal and stone;
Lord of Eternal Life and Light
With Thee there is no death, no night!

8/1/1911

A GOLDEN WEDDING

These fifty years, dear wife, thy love,
Undimmed by any mist of tears,
Has shone with steadfast glow above
The dawn of hopes, the dusk of fears –
                These fifty years.

Along life's road, through night and day,
Thy hands have borne love's bread and wine
Unspilled, unstinted all the way –
God's Alumnus to me and mine,
                These fifty years.

'Twas thine to give and ours to taste
The greater blessing rests on thee,
For thy dear love and thy dear sake
We offer up our hearts – for see
                'Tis fifty years!

Old voices reach us, memories cry
Their greetings mingle in our ears,
Thy children rise and bless thee. I
Have blessed thee all along the years –
                These fifty years.

[Editor's note: Written to Richard's wife Corinna on the occasion of their Golden Wedding celebration. (July 14, 1849-1919)]

THROUGH THE YEARS

Through all the years – since that far summer's day,
    When Love's clear stream in closest union met ;
    To flow, henceforth, a river deeper yet,
And stronger, as its course should find a way
Unto the ocean : where all waters play
    A part in currents swift or slow, or set
    Cross-wise, smooth or rough motion to beget –
Love's life has witness'd, 'Love is life's true stay.'

And through the years they pass'd, (lovingly one),
    Along the common way, filling the plan
        Ordain'd by God to bless the path of life ;

And caring for those things that could be done
        To help life's wearied ones to rise, and scan
            From higher plane order above earth's strife.

July 14, 1869 - 1919

[Editor's note: Believed written for the occasion of their Golden Wedding celebration]

THE TRIO

I had a vision of three poets – one
The Dreamer on the Hill, of days long gone,
And one; crowned singer of today; who fills
The country roads and fields of daffodils
With life and beauty, and the third, whose hands
Write them with the time-defying bands
Of poet-kinship – she, whose feet once trod
Where every bush was seen "afire with God",
And now her own "lost bower" has found again,
Where the lost gold of sunset last has lain.

May 25, 1920

ON MALVERN HILLS
(Alternative version)

On Malvern Hills the hawthorns bloom –
And gold abounds - in gorse and broom –
And fairy-tunes the harebells play,
And kestrels hover all the day :
The sunrise-gleam the valley fills ;
The Cotswolds hail the Malvern Hills.

On Malvern Hills when Summer burns,
To gold and bronze the bracken turns,
And foxgloves rear, in purple state,
Their belfry-spires and linger late :
The plain with sunset-glory thrills ;
The Cotswolds greet the Malvern Hills.

On Malvern Hills the caps of snow
First warn us how the seasons go,
And drifts, with peeping rocks, complete
Their ermine robes from crown to feet ;
Then Winter's "Hush!" each valley stills
To sleep, beneath the Malvern Hills.

On Malvern Hills, 'neath Western skies,
We gaze where wooded heights arise
With peaceful hollows, laughing streams;
Like Langland, there, we dream our dreams
"On a May mornynge." Rapture fills
The hearts that beat on Malvern Hills!

11/12/1921

EVERLASTING FLOWERS

Dear heart, Life's sun and showers;
    The joy of woods and hills;
The scent of new-born flowers;
    The gold of daffodils;

The glow of Summer glory;
    The love that lives and grows;
The old, re-written story;
    The tale without a close;

The Autumn's gathered treasure;
    God's gifts from day to day;
The fuller cup of pleasure; -
    Say, will this flow away?

For, dear, our year is waning;
    The hours have played their parts –
"Nay, Spring is always ripening,
    The flowers are in our hearts."

Dec 21/22

[Editor's note: Probably written to wife Corinna]

HEALING

At the roaring loom of Time I ply
And weave for God the garment that we know him by

The Earth Spirit in Faust

Green of the grass-lands and purple of heather;
    Gold of the broom and the wood's golden-rod:
These are the colours Earth mingles together –
    Taken for the garment she weaves for her God:

Aqua of hare-bells and, when the year waneth,
    Bronze of her bracken to deepen its hue;
Spring's hawthorn snowflakes may fall, yet remaineth
    Autumn's rich tinctures His work to endure.

. . .

Stricken, I stole through the throng pressing round Him,
    (face of his healing for me and for them);
There, unimpeded, I sought for and found Him –
    Groped for His garment and touched but its hem.

Did you ever go a-walking Back-o'-Skinners',
    Back-o'-Skinners' on a Sunday afternoon,
When the merry birds have sung and had their dinner
    And the nightingales waiting for the moon;
        Back-o'-Skinners' in the Springtime o' the year?

30.12.22

[Editor's note: This handwriting was hard to discern in parts.]

THE CRY OF THE HILLS

What is this cry of SOS
   While Earth puts on her greenery?
This piteous cry can be no less
   To me than 'Save our Scenery'!

"Hand holding hand, your town we guard;
   No shock our line displaces;
We take it hard that, for reward
   You turn and scratch our faces.

"We give you health, we give you fame;
   We are your children's nurses.
And you – you rob us without shame
   To fill your gaping purses.

"Heedless, our beauty you defile;
   Our wealth the vandal seizes;
'Tis true enough that 'man is vile'
   The 'prospect' scarcely 'pleases'."

THE REPLY
The cry has sounded far and near;
   The need still needs our backing
Colwall has answered with a cheer,
   And Malvern won't be lacking

March 15, 1924

AFTER MANY YEARS

Is it time, heart of mine, is it so,
That with age all the flame has sunk low;
All the radiance gone from the earth;
All the precious things lessed is worth:
And my heart in swift anger replies
"These, these are the Evil One's lies."

Dear of old, cleaner still as the years roll away,
And the long road is trodden more feebly to-day:
The path's unclear, the future is dim -
God sees all and knows all – we leave it with Him.

Jul 14 & 15, 1927

TO OUR TULIP TREE
(Thornbank School)

Here at the foot of the lawn in your splendour,
   Regally robed with your garment of gold
Gathered about you, in folds of light and tender,
   Wooed by the winds that have loved you of old.

Bearer of blossoms of grace and of wonder;
   Shelter form storm-cloud and shade from the sun;
We shall remember you, though the years sunder
   Us from your presence, when school-days are done.

Games played beneath you, the books that we cherish,
   Friendships cemented and wonderful schemes
Fashioned by fancy – to live or to perish –
   We shall recapture those early day-dreams.

Live on old friend ! and whatever betide us,
   We shall look back to the happy days spent
Here in your keeping, whose kindly leaves hide us
   Safe in the folds of your Summer-spread tent.

September 1928

AFTER MANY DAYS

Love, if ill requited, is it wholly wasted?
   Hidden in its working is it wholly lost?
How can love partaken be as love untasted –
   Prove a vain oblation – seeing what it cost?

Deep within earth's bosom lie the sunbeams sleeping,
   Prisoned with the forests in their silent tomb,
Where the ages hold them, safe within their keeping,
   Till they flash in hearthglow when the time has come.

Gifts of time are passing; need for them may never
   In the years to follow once again arise;
But life's need of love abides with life for ever,
   And it only slumbers where it quiet lies.

AFTER MANY DAYS (Alternative version)

We walked through meadows hand-in-hand;
    We jumped the brook together
We said "This must be fairy-land-"
    We found a ring-doves' feather;

You said 'twas from an angel's wing,
    To drop a blessing o'er us;
I said it marked the track of Spring,
    Who went this way before us:

We trod the pine-woods' solemn aisle,
    Our footsteps scarcely sounded;
We thought we saw a rabbit smile
    As, flag-in-air, he bounded:

And out again, where shone the light,
    We stepped beyond the wood-land
Where lay the gorse-gold common bright,
    Set in its frame of good land.

*****

The years have fled, aye many a year
    And girl and boy no longer
Walk hand-in-hand. What said you, dear,
    "That love grows ever stronger"?

                                  May 2nd, 1929

MAY

The Chestnut's thousand candles are all alight to-day,
And the hedge is dressed with beauty in the bridal-robe of May:

The Cuckoo shouts to tell us that Spring is here again,
And the Yaffle laughs his loudest as he dips across the plain.

And we would go a-Maying and forget the vanished hours,
And gather posies once again of Time's unfading flowers.

May 1930

SONNET ("Not far from every one of us")

Thou art not far from us nor absent; we,
   In blissful moments, catch Thy nameless grace,
   And feel Thy breath upon the lifted face
That questions Nature of her bond with Thee:
And when with sorrow bowed, in agony,
   We turn again to Nature, Thee we trace,
   Thy Presence wholly fills th' unwallèd place
And Thine, expressed by her, the sympathy.
I think, in sunny hours, the warmth and light
   We take as Nature's gift, direct from her,
   And give the first place to Thine almoner,
But when they fail us, and our yearning sight
   Searches for comfort, then, our hearts aver
Thy Face it is makes beautiful the night.

THE COMING OF SPRING

The birds are all a-building, the flowers all a-blowing,
The clouds move like an argosy that out to sea is going;
The bluebells trembling belfry with many changes fills,
And lifted golden trumpets sound the notes of daffodils;
And rainbows in the valley, and glints of sun and rain,
Proclaim the yearly miracle – that Spring is here again.

VITA NUOVA (The First Buttercup)

This is Earth's token of a life renewed –
   While yet the grim frost binds her, and the snow
   Lingers within her shadow, she would show
Her stillness was but Death's similitude.

Swiftly her fairy-prince drew nigh and wooed
   With sunny kisses, waking her and lo!
   Here, on her breast, she placed his colour, so
To gladden him, whose love her love pursued.

O little flower, apparelled like the day,
   Thou bringest visions of the golden fields
   Of summer, breathing perfume; song and mirth
Of children tumbled in the flying hay;
   All flowers; all fruits; all gladness Nature yields,
   And sends us by the love-awakened Earth!

I was surprised to see a plant of the creeping crowfoot (*Ranunculus repens*) in flower on February 26th, before the frost was out of the soil, and white patches of snow were still unmelted.

A HOME RULER (THE CRISIS)

Our thoughts are but of him; our hearts are bowed
    Our voices sink to whispers; he is great,
    Nigh infinite in power : affairs of state,
We counted first, scarce second are allowed,
For he has conquered. All the tiny crowd
    Of leal people love him – awe-touched, wait
    A word to-morrow, heavy with the fate
Of him and all, who serving him are proud.
This is our true home-ruler; he who gives
    Such promise of a future. Ah! dear friends,
    One look, one smile, we long for! One who tends
Him skilfully, and loves him, with us grieves.
    Tom-morrow he will tell us – God, Who sends
All good, will let him tell us – " Baby lives".

AT THE ROLL OF HONOUR

These are the cherished names of those who died
And, dying, saved us. We salute them here
In grateful silence, lacking fitter words!
One in relentless purpose were they all;
One in the fellowship of righteous war.

These are the men who loved our guardian hills;
Whose eyes were lifted to them; who, perchance,
Nourished beneath their shadow, at their feet,
Drew steadfastness from their eternal calm
And strength from their strength. We shall not forget.
But, for our children and the yet unborn
The Roll remains; to them, our legacy
Of names we hold in honour, and believe,
Beyond all time, within God's timeless world,
Where the white stone and the new name are given,
In His uncrumbling archives rest secure.

O stricken hearts, faint not! You have not lost
Your dear ones; you, in loving faith, have laid
Your gifts upon God's Altar, wet with tears.

LOVE'S CRY (Unpublished version)

If I should ever spread my arms in vain.
Mocked by a mirage of departed years,
And sodden rapture turn to sodden tears,
And lips, unmated, piteously complain;
Let not her peace be broken by my pain,
Nor loss be loss, where she, amid her peers,
A music born of silence ever hears
In valleys where old sunsets long have lain.

Love, thou hast helped me in the years gone by!
How shall I help thee in the days that are?
May God transmute to prayer each wailing cry,
And grief as gladness reach thee from afar;
Till earthward falls the glory of thy star
And Death in light and life reveals thee nigh.

THE COMFORT

Here to the wayside thistle flashing down
Like flakes of Heaven's run thee, the butterflies
Unfold their wings across the purple dips,
Or lift them and reveal soft grey and brown:
In hot haste now (but can he win renown?)
To wrest possession of their hurried prize
Another claimant, being veiled, hits,
And little rapes o'er the thistles' crown.

What lesson? Surely none, yet would we gaze
On life and beauty while the seasons roll,
And watching Nature's doings, learn her ways,
Look on the workings of her mighty soul.
So win some secret from the countless whole
Thankful for God's gift of summer days

RFT

Comfortingly – one small Copper of the Common Miel Butterflies.

[Editor's note: This handwriting was hard to discern in parts.]

(Title unknown)

We laid him in God's garden
    In the forenoon of the year —
    All in life we held most dear.

Speed's the year? Aye, gone's the Summer
    Gone the dread of Winter's chill —
    Summer's sun shines somewhere still.

Autumn's fall our grief must mellow,
    Steadfast Faith supplant Regret —
    Time Triumphant triumphs yet.

Winter — welcome Winter's advent,
    Winter — Death — where is thy sting?
    When Winter comes, God grant us Spring.

THE ABBEY SCHOOL

Ora, labora, lude – school motto

Here, where the Hills lie in fold after fold,
And two counties climb up them and meet,
Where, in broom and in gorse-woven garments of gold,
    They guard o'er the plain at their feet –

Here our School clusters her houses, all swathed
    In the early-morn of sun;
And here in the coolness of eventide bathed
    When the tale of our lessons is done:

Fair fields for our games stretch out to the East –
    Our Umpires, the Hills of the West –
Here we all "play the game," the Head Girl and the least,
    And each for her side does her best:

Above, our own Chapel lies nestled in peace –
    The peace she invites us to share –
Where sorrows should lighten and worries should cease,
    In the Home of our praise and our prayer:

The Junior House starts us well on our way;
    At Shelsley, in serious mood,
We work for "exams" at the French House all day,
    Our dear mother-tongue is tabooed:

At Heathlands we learn how to cook and to sew,
        To answer the door and the 'phone,
And a hundred and one things good housewives should know
        When they set up a home of their own:

The "Gym" finds a place for athletics and drill;
        Song and dance have their home in the Hall,
Where at Lectures and Plays all the many seats fill
        'Neath our Head looking down from the wall.

So we pray, work and play while the term slips away,
        And at times, for a break in our study,
A Field Club excursion demands a half-day
        And sends us home hungry and muddy.

[Editor's note: This typed poem was found in one of RFT's notebooks and whilst it is not signed or initialled by him – confirming his authorship – it is undoubtedly in his style, so I have no reason to think it is not his work.]

ONE OF LIFE'S PICTURES

Bless'd union of lives: Through years more strong
That common love touch'd common joys and pain.

A lovely thing: Which, all the way along –
    When skies were blue; and when the mists of rain
Veil'd the white road, and all the birds of song
    Their silence kept; or, when some joyous strain
Made glad your hearts – found its true place among
    Life's canvases of beauty that remain.

[Editor's note: This typed poem was found in one of RFT's notebooks and whilst it is not signed or initialled by him – confirming his authorship – it is undoubtedly in his style, so I have no reason to think it is not his work.]

THE MUSIC OF THE YEARS

As through the years, so on this gladsome day,
    That deepest fullest note again shall sound:
Recalling sacred hopes each heart did lay
    Upon the altar, which your faith had found
E'en where you walk'd, along the common way
    (Which should henceforth to you be hallow'd ground)
Where you should know that love is life's true stay;
    And learn its music, as the years came round.

[Editor's note: This typed poem was found in one of RFT's notebooks and whilst it is not signed or initialled by him – confirming his authorship – it is undoubtedly in his style, so I have no reason to think it is not his work.]

Healing.

> At the roaring loom of Time I ply
> And weave for God the garment that we know Him by
>
> *The Earth Spirit in Faust.*

Green of the grass-lands and purple of heather;
Gold of the broom and the wood's golden-rod:
These are the colours Earth mingles together —
Takes for the garment she weaves for her God:

Azure of blue-bells and, when the year waneth,
Bronze of the bracken to deepen its hue;
Spring's hawthorn snowflakes may fall, yet remaineth
Autumn's rich tincture, this robe to endue.

Stricken, I stole through the throng pressing round Him,
(Sure of His healing for me and for them);
There, unregarded, I sought for and found Him —
Groped for His garment and touched but its hem.

Everlasting Flowers

Dear heart, Life's sun and showers;
    The joy of woods and hills;
The scent of new-born flowers;
    The gold of daffodils;

The glow of summer glory;
    The love that lives and grows;
The old, re-written story;
    The tale without a close;

The Autumn's gathered treasure;
    God's gifts from day to day;
The fuller cup of pleasure; —
    Say, will they pass away?

For, dear, our year is waning;
    Its blooms have played their parts —
"Nay, Spring is always reigning,
    The flowers are in our hearts."

                        Dec 21/22

A Golden Wedding.
(July, 14. 1869–1919.)

These fifty years, dear wife, thy love,
  Undimmed by any mist of tears,
Has shone with steadfast glow above
  The dawn of hopes, the dusk of fears —
        These fifty years.

Along Life's road, through night and day,
  Thy hands have borne Love's bread and wine
Unspilled, unstinted all the way —
  God's Almoner to me and mine,
        These fifty years.

'Twas thine to give and mine to take,
  The greater blessing rests on thee,
For thy dear love and thy dear sake
  We offer up our hearts — for see
        'Tis fifty years!

Old voices reach us, new ones cry,
  Their greetings mingle in our ears,
Thy children rise and bless thee. I
  Have blessed thee all along the years —
        These fifty years.
                                R.

DIAMOND WEDDING.

Celebration at the Wells.

Congratulations from the King and Queen.

"I am commanded to convey to you both the hearty congratulations of the King and Queen on the happy occasion of your Diamond Wedding. Their Majesties trust that you may be spared to one another to enjoy the blessings of health and contentment for many years."

Thus ran a telegram from Buckingham Palace, signed by the King's Private Secretary, on the occasion of the Diamond Wedding of Mr. and Mrs. R. F. Towndrow, of Ashville, Malvern Wells, celebrated on Sunday last. Aged 83 and 81 respectively, the venerable couple are wonderfully well for their years. They were married on July 14th, 1869, at Westbury-on-Trym, near Bristol, and took up residence at Malvern Link, where they remained for 40 years, and since then have lived at Malvern Wells. On the auspicious occasion in question, they were the recipients of many telegrams and messages of congratulation, and were blessed with the presence of five of their six sons, one of whom is in Canada. They have thirteen grand-children and one great grand-daughter.

Mr. Towndrow is well-known in the Midlands. He is a botanist and an Associate of the Linnean Society; a member of the Malvern Hills Conservators, the Geographical Society, the Malvern Higher Education Committee, and the Committee of the Malvern Field Club. Mr. Towndrow is also a School Manager in connection with the Malvern Link and Malvern Wells Church Schools.

About The Editor

Chris Towndrow has been a writer for over thirty years.

His initial creative efforts were in poetry during the late 1980s, and then short stories. After his first detective novella in 1991, he began writing science fiction novels, inspired by Isaac Asimov, Iain M Banks, and numerous film and TV canons.
Following a brief spell producing screenplays in several genres, he moved into playwriting and has had a number of productions professionally performed.
Since 2004, Chris has written and published multiple genres of novels and short stories, including absurd comedy, hard sci-fi, historical fiction, contemporary drama, cosy mystery and romantic comedy.

He lives in outer London with his family and works as a video editor and producer. He is a member of the UK Society Of Authors.

Visit his website at: www.christowndrow.co.uk

www.ingramcontent.com/pod-product-compliance
Lightning Source LLC
Chambersburg PA
CBHW031100080526
44587CB00011B/765